DFB brass helmet 1866-1937

Contents

Front cover: Captain John Myers at the YMCA fire, O'Connell Street.
(Courtesy of the National Library of Ireland).

List of Abbreviations

ADRIC	Auxiliary Division Royal Irish Constabulary
ASC	Army Service Corps
ASU	Active Service Unit
BMH	Bureau of Military History
DFB	Dublin Fire Brigade
DFBU	Dublin Firebrigademen's Union
DMP	Dublin Metropolitan Police
DTC	Dublin Trades Council
ICA	Irish Citizen Army
IRA	Irish Republican Army
KPM	King's Police Medal
RIC	Royal Irish Constabulary

Dedication

In memory of my parents, Patrick and Sarah Fallon,
who passed on to us their love of Ireland,
and the stories of our land.

But oh the days are soft
Soft enough to forget
the lesson better learnt
The bullet on the wet streets
The crooked deal
The steel behind the laugh
The Four Courts burnt

Dublin **by Louis MacNeice**

Acknowledgements

THANKS are due to many people and institutions for their generous help and assistance with this project. My deep and sincere thanks to Sile Coleman, Colette Allen, David Power and all at South Dublin Libraries Local Studies section for taking this book on board and supporting it. To Denis A Cronin, M.A. of the Department of History, NUIM, for his guidance and support. To my longstanding friends, fire service historians and authors Tom Geraghty and Pat Poland. To author and historian of the Irish Revolution, Liz Gillis, for her invaluable help and generosity in making her research available to me. To Mike Connolly for sharing his research on his uncle, Joseph Connolly. To Colm Smart and Vincent Rogers for sharing their family history and giving me access to family papers and photographs. To the Purcell family and especially Peter and Michael, for allowing me access to Captain Thomas Purcell's personal records. To the Doyle family for allowing me access to Edward Doyle's medals and photos. To Martin Thompson of the Fire Service Trust for his constant help and for the work he does in preserving our fire service heritage. To Liam O Luanaigh for expertise and access to his extensive files and research. To Des Durkin for his friendship and support. To the Fitzpatrick family, especially Eamonn, Danny (snr) and Danny (jnr). To Billy Redmond and Paddy Kelly for giving me access to their father's records and for their generous help. To the Carroll family for allowing me to read and copy the papers and photos left to them by their father, Billy Carroll. To historians Shane MacThomáis and Paul O'Brien for their unstinting support and encouragement for this project. To James Langton, Michael Whelan, Gretta Halpin, Geraldine Mulvaney and Vera Dent.

To my friends and colleagues past and present, at Dolphin's Barn fire station and especially to all on C watch for their support and friendship. To Third Officer Terry Kearney and Ms Breeda Melvin of the Dublin Fire Brigade for allowing me access to material in the DFB Museum for this book and for their support and assistance to me during my time as curator there.

To Comdt. Victor Laing (retired), Military Archives, Cathal Brugha Barracks, for his generous help and to all the staff at Military Archives who do such good and valuable work. To Mary Clarke and the staff of the Dublin City Archives, Pearse Street. To Treasa Harkin of the Irish Traditional Music Archive. To the Police Museum, Belfast. To all at the Irish Volunteers Commemorative Orgainisation. To the staff of the National Library of Ireland, the National Archives of Ireland and the National Photographic Archive.

Most of all my wife Maria and our sons, Donal and Luke for their patience, understanding, help and support.

My grateful thanks to all who put their shoulder to the wheel.

Foreword

DUBLIN Fire Brigade is this year celebrating 150 years of service to the people of Dublin so this short book is a welcome piece on two particular but historic aspects of the actions of those who served in the Brigade. Since its humble beginnings in 1862 it has been an institution with flaws like most organisations but throughout its existence its firefighters have given civic service of the highest commitment at all times when the people of Dublin most needed it. From the beginning it has been more than a fire service, it has in fact been the emergency service for the people and their city. Its members have bravely faced fires, bombs, shelling, shooting, floods, collapsing tenements, train crashes, ship fires, drownings and death or injury to colleagues on duty, yet their role has received scant mention in the histories of the city.

The decision in 1862 by the then Dublin corporation to form a Municipal Fire Service was a political statement at a time when moves were afoot to create a Police Fire Service as existed in Belfast and other cities in the U.K. Unlike these other cities however where the police was controlled by the elected council, the Dublin Metropolitan Police was a Castle controlled organisation paid for by Corporation rates. With its early beginings in a Corporation yard in Winetavern Street and a small converted area at the rear of the former City Hall in South William Street it struggled to provide adequate fire and emergency cover in a port city with hundreds of tenement houses, basement factories and various industries, a city short of funds because its middle classes had abandoned the squalor for Clontarf, Pembroke, Rathmines and Rathgar. Its first Chief Fire Officer was a recently returned Irishman from New York at a time when many arriving Irish Americans were considered as likely Fenians or sympathisers.

In 1892 when this story really begins the Brigade was undergoing major change and expansion under a new Chief Fire Officer, Captain Purcell, a man with ability and vision for building a service that would compare with any in the U.K, with modern stations, equipment, trained and disciplined firemen. Many of those employed maintained their former trade union membership from previous employment. Now in an organised environment living in the fire stations they realised the need to protect themselves from exploitation and forty-three (from a total of forty-four) of them formed the Dublin Firemens Union. The DFB became the first trade union organised fire service in Europe.

Over the next twenty years under Captains Purcell's leadership new modern fire stations strategically placed provided proper fire cover in the city. Horse drawn steamers replaced obsolete manual pumps and fire escape ladders manned twenty-four hours a day were set in central locations in the city.

In 1898 the Brigade acquired its first horse drawn ambulance and all firemen were trained in first aid. From 1912 onwards horses were being replaced by motor driven vehicles with petrol driven fire pumps and the escape ladders were replaced with street fire alarms.

Much painstaking research has been undertaken by the author, Las Fallon, to compile the latter half of this history. It shows a group of serving men who, while carrying out their normal duties in the period 1913/1922, involved themselves directly in deed not rhetoric in the national struggle for independence. This was the period when the Dublin Fire Brigade established a reputation second to none in commitment on fire and ambulance as the city was in continuous turmoil with baton charges, shooting, shelling, curfews and gigantic conflagrations. The role of the men of the DFB throughout this momentous period in Irish history is largely ignored and forgotten by historians so this book in a small way tries to redress this omission both on behalf of those who served but also those who contributed in no small way in the independence struggle. That was an era of shared sacrifice by the people of Ireland to overthrow imperialism and establish democracy.

Tom Geraghty

Introduction

I joined the Dublin Fire Brigade as a recruit firefighter in 1985. I had become part of an organisation with its own special niche in the history of Dublin. I was always interested in history, especially Irish history and in particular the story of that amazing generation who fought for our freedom in the revolution. Within the Brigade I became aware of our own particular history. I worked with men who had fought the fire when the British Embassy was burned after Bloody Sunday in 1972, who had dealt with the awful aftermath of the 1974 car bombings in the city and some who, in more recent years, had rescued the living and recovered the dead from the Stardust Disco.

When I joined, the most senior firefighters and officers had been in the service since the 1950s. They in their turn had been recruits when the senior men in the brigade had seen service during the Belfast blitz and the North Strand bombing. Many of the men with whom they worked vividly remembered the loss of three firefighters in the Pearse Street tragedy of 1936 when Bob Malone, Tom Nugent and Peter McArdle lost their lives in a building collapse at a tenement fire.

Going back further, the fathers and grandfathers of men I worked with had fought the fires at Easter 1916 and had been eyewitnesses to history during the years of the revolution. The fathers of others had taken part in that revolution. There were scraps of stories from those years – a folklore, a half remembered history. When I set out on this project it was a journey to recover this lost history.

The aim of this book is to examine and bring into the public domain evidence of co-operation between members of the Dublin Fire Brigade (DFB)[1] and the intelligence branches of the Irish Republican Army (IRA) and Irish Citizen Army (ICA) during the period from the 1916 Rising to the early days of the Civil War.

---

[1]While the official name has been Dublin Fire Brigade since 1862, Dublin Fire Department, Dublin Corporation Fire Brigade, Dublin City Fire Brigade, City Fire Brigade and Dublin Metropolitan Fire Brigade were also used on official documents during the period covered by this study, Dublin Fire Brigade or DFB will be used at all times in this work.

The basic contention of this study is that, in the period under review, members of the DFB operated as *de facto* members of the intelligence service of both the IRA and the ICA. Individual DFB members were also active members of the IRA and the ICA and used their positions within the DFB to facilitate IRA operations. In fact they were complicit in some of the major operations of the War of Independence in Dublin. The examination of the involvement of members of the Dublin Fire Brigade, a uniformed, disciplined body of public servants in effectively subverting the state throws a modest light on an unexamined facet of the period.

The foundation of trade unionism within the DFB from the 1890s will also be examined as will the struggle to improve both working and living conditions for the city's firemen. This led them at times into conflict with both the Chief Fire Officer, Captain Purcell, and with the Waterworks Committee of Dublin Corporation, who ran the Brigade at that time. The establishment of the Dublin Fire Brigademen's Union (DFBU) in 1892 led to the involvement of the firefighters in the trade union organisation of the city. The DFB was in fact the first fire brigade in the British Isles to be unionised. By 1913 the DFBU, although not involved directly in the Lockout, was an active member of the Dublin Trades Council and was considered by members of the Dublin Metropolitan Police (DMP) to be a politicised body.[2] It can be argued that the firemen's trade union background and experience made them more open to the ideals of the Republican movement.

1892 is the starting point both because of its significance as the first year in which firemen were represented by a trade union and also because that year brought a new chief officer to Dublin. Thomas Purcell, 'the Captain', turned Dublin's fire brigade from a provincial service of limited importance within the British fire service, of which it was then part, into one of the foremost brigades within that service. He was always at the cutting edge of new technology in firefighting and many of the innovations he championed were his own inventions.

---

[2]David Nelligan, *The spy in the Castle* (London, 1968), pp. 51-2.

The story of the involvement of members of the DFB in the War of Independence has not been covered in any previous work. While the history of the Irish fire service has been brilliantly documented in recent years by historians such as Tom Geraghty and Pat Poland, both of whose work is referred to in this book, no separate study of the brigade in the revolutionary period has yet been written.

The main sources used for the study were statements made to the Bureau of Military History (BMH) in the 1948-1958 period by participants, including some firemen. Statements made under the Military Service Pensions Act were also used but these are not in the public domain to anything like the extent that BMH statements are. I would like to thank the families of the men involved for permission to quote from the pension statements. The planned release of this pension material will be a huge boon to historians and will, in conjunction with the Bureau of Military History material already available, provide a massive insight into the role of many of the often overlooked participants, big and small.

As the study examines the role of undercover agents of a secret army in a war situation, records are understandably scarce. However some participants did write and speak of their involvement and material was located in the possession of the families of some of these men. Contemporary newspapers, including American papers aimed at the Irish community in the United States, provided some new material which proved of great interest.

Relevant photographs are used throughout. Wherever possible these are previously unpublished or certainly not published since the period under review. Some are posed group or individual photos, some are 'action' shots taken by press photographers and one is a newly discovered posed propaganda photo of Dublin firemen from the Chicago Tribune, a paper with a large Irish American readership.

There is a considerable body of published work on the 1916-1923 period available and this was used to provide background information on the national context of the story being told. For the earlier period a number of works on the insurance industry and the early fire offices and on fire service history were consulted as were works on social conditions and housing in Dublin in the nineteenth and twentieth centuries.

In the first chapter the origins of organised firefighting in Dublin are examined. The story of how the service developed from being a function of the local parish to a full municipal service is explained. The background to the formation of the Dublin Fire Brigade is examined and a brief synopsis of its early years is provided. The DFB of the late nineteenth century is examined in the second chapter. The origins of trade unionism within the DFB are discussed and the gradual growth of trade unionism and organised labour is traced by successive memorials outlining the working and living conditions of the city's firemen. In the following chapters the role of the Brigade during the Easter Rising and the War of Independence is covered. In these chapters the emerging resistance to British rule and the part played by members of the DFB in that resistance is discussed and examined. Relying heavily on primary source material, the role of a number of firemen is illustrated. The last chapter deals with the events of the Civil War in Dublin with the main emphasis on the battle for Dublin and the events surrounding it from a fire service perspective. A conclusion and list of appendices will attempt to tie up the various strands of information and narrative and provide an overview of the project.

This is a story of, and from, Dublin and is just one very small part of the mosaic that makes up the history of this city and county. It is a story of men who served the people of Dublin always, and who, when times called for it, put themselves in harm's way to serve their country's cause.

I can only hope that I have done justice to their memory and helped to preserve their story.

CHAPTER I

The origins of organised firefighting in Dublin

DUBLIN Fire Brigade was founded following an Act of Parliament in 1862. The formation of a municipal brigade to protect the city was calculated to address the issue of a lack of a single firefighting force for Dublin. Prior to this the firefighting arrangements for the city were, to say the least, fragmented and without central leadership or control.

18th Century parish fire engine of St. Werburghs parish *(Photo author).*

For many years the main firefighting unit in the city was the Church of Ireland parish fire engines or 'parish pumps' each under the control of the parish beadle. The onus to keep and maintain these engines originated in an act of George 1 in 1715 (2 George 1), while a second act of 1719 (6 George 1) specified that each parish must maintain one large and one small engine and associated gear.[1] The corporation had itself purchased a fire engine in 1711 and had engaged one John Oates 'to keep in order the water engine belonging to the city and cause six men once a quarter,

---

[1]Pat Poland, *For whom the bells tolled: a history of Cork fire services, 1622-1900* (Dublin, 2010), p.47.

at his own expense, to play on the said engine'.[2] The engine ordered in 1711 may be said to be the origin of a municipal fire brigade but in reality it was more of a gesture towards protecting the city with the main onus falling on the parish engines. Each parish where a fire occurred made a payment to the first, second and third engine to arrive at the scene of the fire. Payment was based on time of arrival at the fire rather than the application of water to it. Poorer parishes often cut back on maintenance of the engine as the requirement was to attend the fire in their own parish or an adjoining one, not to play an effective part in extinguishing it.

Following the Great Fire of London in 1666, the question of a system to compensate property owners for the loss of buildings and their contents had arisen. In London Nicholas Barbon set up the Fire Office 'at the backside of the Royal Exchange' in 1680.[3] This was the first fire insurance company and, for a short time, had a monopoly but competitors soon appeared. In London, where the early offices were based, the companies had recruited Thames watermen, independent contractors who worked on the river and who were considered to be strong and agile and suited to the new trade of 'waterman-fireman' (soon shortened to fireman). Each company recruited a crew of firemen who were trained up to use the manual engines of the period. These relied on relays of volunteers pumping water through the engines by use of handles attached to levers which the pumpers worked up and down to draw water from a cistern within the engine. This was fed by either a bucket chain or, if drawing from an open source, by means of a leather suction hose or 'sucking worm'. The fire brigade of each company was advertised for the exclusive use of its customers and the companies made much of the availability of the latest engines in constant readiness to serve and protect their customers. While the initial idea was for the company brigade to service the company's customers only, they soon co-operated to deal with any insured property and later to deal with any fire in the locality in order to demonstrate their efficiency.

[2]Pat Poland, *For whom the bells tolled: a history of Cork fire services, 1622-1900* (Dublin, 2010), p.47.

[3]Tom Geraghty and Trevor Whitehead, *The Dublin Fire Brigade a history of the brigade, the fires and the emergencies* (Dublin 2004), pp. 2-3.

Hibernian Insurance Company firemark. The Hibernian was the first Irish fire assurance company, founded in 1771 which was later bought over by the Sun Assurance in 1839.

National Assurance Company firemark, founded in 1822. Both companies maintained fire brigades in Dublin.

Each company supplied their firemen with uniforms, in a variety of colours and patterns, designed not for protection or serviceability but rather to enhance the company's image. In the same way each company marked the wall of insured properties with a colourful firemark made of lead with the company emblem and the policy number embossed on to it. No property was considered insured until fitted with its firemark, an important consideration in an era before the penny post and the universal use of house numbers to indicate addresses.

The insurance companies prospered and soon had their eyes set on potential business across the Irish Sea. The first insurance office to set up in Ireland was the Royal Exchange Assurance (REA founded in 1720) which appointed an Irish agent, Luke Gaven, and set up an Irish office in Dublin in 1722.[4] The REA offered their customers the use of the company fire brigade as did the other companies which followed them into the Irish market. It is believed that seventeen insurance companies maintained fire engine establishments (fire brigades) in the city by the early nineteenth century and in effect the insurance company's fire engines were the city's fire service.[5] In 1854 Dublin Corporation purchased two fire engines, one for the use of the Dublin Metropolitan Police to be based at their depot in Kevin Street and one for the corporation's own 'fire extinction depot' at Whitehorse Yard off Winetavern Street. Whitehorse Yard was manned by corporation workers who carried on their normal duties with the waterworks department but who had received training on the fire engines and could turn out with them to any fire day or night (the part time firemen lived in houses at numbers 5 and 6 Cook Street). The Dublin Metropolitan Police (DMP) also responded to fires in the city by using recruits from their depot in Kevin Street and members of the DMP's mounted troop to man the engine under the command of a depot sergeant who had received instruction in using the engine.[6] Each military barracks in the city also

---

[4]Barry Supple, *The Royal Exchange Assurance, a history of British insurance 1720-1970* (London, 1970), p.98.
[5]Geraghty and Whitehead, The Dublin fire brigade, p.9.
[6]Jim Herlihy, The Dublin Metropolitan Police (Dublin 2001), pp 86-7.

had fire fighting apparatus up to and including manual engines, which were manned by a fire picket drawn from the garrison. These could, by arrangement, turn out to fires if needed. A more regular use for the troops was for them to be turned out to assist with crowd control and to help man the engines at major fires in the city. A full size manual engine could require up to twenty men to operate the levers and pump the engine. It was exhausting work and required relays of men to be available to keep the engine working. The other source of fire engines available to the city was from private brigades in the various breweries, distilleries, factories and institutions which maintained their own engines in response to the inherent risks of their trade. The role of the insurance fire brigades was purely to protect property and they carried no ladders or fire escapes to help save lives. If lives were saved by the insurance firemen it was incidental to the protection of insured property which was the role their employers paid them for.

Some of the axes used by firemen in the course of duty.

Late 18th Century firemark of the Royal Exchange Assurance. Established in London in 1720, they set up a branch and fire brigade in Dublin in 1722.

Sun Fire Office firemark issued c1810. The sun fire engine was an integral part of Dublin's fire protection until the establishment of the municipal fire brigade.

The system was chaotic and without central control and after a series of fires in the city the focus of attention on the lack of a properly organised municipal fire and rescue service came to a head on the night of 11 November 1860. A fire in the Kildare Street Club, a bastion of the ruling class, took the lives of three women and destroyed the premises. Nine people were rescued by the actions of a bystander who entered the building and led them to safety across the rooftops. The response to the fire included 200 soldiers of the 96th regiment, St. Ann's parish engine (which was found to be useless), the Whitehorse Yard engine, the DMP engine, St. Mark's parish engine and the insurance company engines. No fire escape ladder was brought to the scene of the fire. Much criticism was levelled at all concerned due to many of the engines present having different sized couplings, which meant that they could not supply each other with water, and with the difficulty of finding a water supply at all. The Kildare Street Club fire and a number of other destructive fires in the city around that time led to calls for a properly organised municipal fire brigade, with adequate training and equipment, to be set up under the control of Dublin Corporation. The Waterworks Committee considered the proposal and over the following year held a series of meetings and considered a number of proposals and points of view. The Dublin Corporation Waterworks Act of 1861 enabled a public water rate to be levied. Part of the proceeds of this rate was to be used to fund the cost and expenses of a public fire brigade. A bill was formulated and put forward to parliament. The Dublin Corporation Fire Brigade Act 1862 (25 Victoria c 38) received the Royal Assent on 3 June 1862 and the Dublin Fire Brigade was established from that date and became operational in September of that year.

The first municipal fire brigade in these islands had been set up in Edinburgh in 1824 while in Ireland the city of Belfast had a municipal fire service from 1841 (albeit under the control of the Belfast Police which, like the DMP, were an autonomous force at that time).[7]

---

[7]The Belfast police were under the control of the Belfast City Council, unlike the DMP which was run by Dublin Castle and outside the control of Dublin Corporation. This was a very sore point for the Corporation which was forced to fund the DMP but had no say in its operations.

It should be noted that London did not have municipal control of its fire service until the insurance office controlled London Fire Engine Establishment was replaced by the Metropolitan Fire Brigade on 1 January 1866 by Parliament (28 & 29 Victoria c 90).[8]

The man chosen to lead the new Dublin Fire Brigade was Robert Ingram, an Irishman who had lived in New York for ten years. Ingram, an engraver by trade, had served as a member of the fire department in New York. New York, like other American cities at the period, had a volunteer fire department and to be one of the 'fire laddies' was considered to be a major social accomplishment. Ingram was a member of the Niagara No. 2 Hose Company based in Lower Manhattan.

Theatre Royal fire, 1880. Illustrated London News *(Author's collection)*.

[8]Sally Holloway, *London's noble fire brigades 1833-1904* (London, 1973), p.45.

8

When Robert Ingram returned to Dublin to take up his new post, he brought a little of the New York fire scene with him. He dressed his men in a uniform quite unlike that of any British fire service of the period. They wore red flannel shirts in imitation of the New York Fire Department and also the kepi headgear of the U.S Army. Officers of the new Dublin brigade wore a uniform which was a copy of that worn by officers of the U.S Federal Army. The only concession to British fire brigade uniform came after 1866 when the brigade adopted the British style brass helmet which itself had been developed by a Cork man, Eyre Massey Shaw, chief officer of the Metropolitan Fire Brigade in London.[9]

Ingram served as Chief Officer until his death on 15 May 1882. His period of office had seen the brigade grow as an emergency service and he had fought the city's fires, both large and small. The brigade was based at two stations in those years, the headquarters in Coppinger Row, off South William Street, and the old depot at Whitehorse Yard. There were also seven street escape stations in the city centre where large wheeled ladders were kept to assist in removing people in danger from fire and to assist the firemen in gaining access to tall buildings. These posts were manned at night by a fireman whose duty it was, in the event of a fire, to notify the nearest fire station of the outbreak and to bring the ladder to the scene of the fire. As the ladders were too unwieldy to be manoeuvred by one man, the fireman could call on policemen or civilians to assist him in bringing it to the scene of the fire.[10] It was preferable from the Corporation's point of view to use policemen if possible as civilians were entitled to be paid for this assistance whereas it was considered part of the duty of the DMP to assist at fires.[11]

---

[9] Neil Wallington; *In case of fire: The illustrated history and modern role of the London fire brigade* (Huddersfield, 2005).

[10] The Waterworks Committee insisted that men on this duty should be dressed in their red shirts regardless of the weather conditions. The men were subject to the wet and cold of Irish winters and requests to allow extra clothing to be worn were refused. This led to health problems and even resignations of firemen in the early years due to the hardship involved.

[11] The DMP objected strongly to being used for operating pumps or ladders at fires feeling that their duty ran to crowd control only.

During Ingram's period of office the brigade had faced major fires, including those in Westmoreland Street in 1866, the great Liberties whiskey fire of 1875, Jacobs biscuit factory fire of 1880 and the Theatre Royal fire of 1880, each of which strained the resources of the brigade to breaking point. Along with these there were many small outbreaks in the slums and tenements which were such a feature of central Dublin in that period.[12] The city as protected by the DFB at that time was basically the city within the canals. The townships which existed outside this area did not pay rates to Dublin Corporation or contribute to the running costs of the corporation fire brigade. In fact two of the townships, Rathmines and Pembroke, maintained their own full time fire brigades

Clayton wheeled street escape ladder. Dublin, 1872.
(Photos courtesy DFB Museum)

[12]Jacinta Prunty, *Dublin Slums 1800-1924: a study in urban geography* (Dublin, 1998), pp 14-5.

10

which had an uneasy and troubled relationship with the DFB until eventually amalgamated with it when the city boundaries were redrawn in 1930. [13]

Liberties Whiskey Fire, 1875. *Illustrated London News (Author's collection).*

Robert Ingram died in 1882 of 'consumption', as tuberculosis was then known, a very common cause of death among Dublin firemen in the early years of the brigade.[14] After his death the position of chief superintendent of the Dublin Fire Brigade was advertised and the position was awarded to John Boyle who had been lieutenant of the brigade since 1868, having previously held a position with the Dublin Metropolitan Police.[15]

---

[13]Seamas Ó Maitiu, *Dublin's suburban towns, 1834-1930* (Dublin, 2003), pp 105-7.

[14]Thomas Purcell, *Statistics of the Dublin Corporation fire brigade department for thirty-four years from its formation September,1862, to 31st December 1895* (Dublin, 1896), p.9.
Reproduced as Appendix C.

[15]Boyle's position within the police is unclear. He is not listed on the personnel files of the DMP which are held in the Garda Museum. Research by the author has shown that he was not an officer in the DMP as previously believed.

On 20 March 1884 fireman John Kite was killed while working at a fire at 10 Trinity Street when part of the building collapsed, burying him in the ruins. He was the first fatality in the line of duty from within the ranks of the brigade. Two more were to die on 20 May 1891 when Inspector Christopher Doherty, a decorated officer with over twenty-five years service and recruit fireman Peter Burke, just three months in the service, were killed when the ladder on which they were working collapsed while they were assisting in the rescue of trapped persons at a fire in 30 Westmoreland Street.[16]

Boyle retired at the end of 1891, a popular chief officer who appears to have been well liked by his men and during whose tenure the brigade had expanded. His period in office was, however, dogged by bad luck and had witnessed the first deaths in service of Dublin firefighters. A major report into the running of the brigade was commissioned and changes were called for. Those changes were going to start in 1892 with the arrival of a new chief officer, Thomas Purcell.

Captain Boyle (in top hat) with Shand Mason steamer and firemen at Whitehorse Yard c1890. *(Photo: DFB Museum).*

[16]Report of the Waterworks Committee, Dublin Corporation annual report 1891, Vol. iii, pp. 513-20.

CHAPTER 2

Origins of Trade Unionism within the DFB

FOLLOWING the Westmoreland Street fire John O'Meara, chairman of the Waterworks Committee and Spencer Harty, City Engineer, travelled to a number of brigades in England and Scotland in order to review their systems of work and draw up new rules and regulations for the Dublin Fire Brigade.[1]

At this time the staff of the DFB consisted of one chief officer, three officers, two engineers (in charge of the horse drawn Shand Mason steam fire engines), three drivers responsible for driving the engines and the care and upkeep of the horses and stables, and thirty-eight firemen. Pay rates started at 21s per week for drivers and firemen in their first year, 23s in their second year and 24s in their third year with a maximum rate of 25s after ten years. Engineers were paid 32s per week.[2] Members of the Brigade could also be awarded chevrons to be worn on their uniform to signify that they had saved a life. Each chevron carried an increase in pay of 1s per week and members could be awarded a maximum of three chevrons.

At this time twenty- three unmarried men lived in the new headquarters station in Clarendon Row and the twenty-two married men lived in rooms in houses in Cook Street and Winetavern Street and these men were based at Winetavern Street station (Whitehorse Yard).

Following an open competition Thomas Purcell was appointed as chief of the brigade.[3] Purcell was born in Kilkenny in 1851 and was a civil engineer by profession. He had served as a volunteer fireman in Kilkenny

---

[1] Report of the Waterworks Committee, *Dublin Corporation annual report, 1891,* vol. i, pp 443-4.
[2] Sean Redmond, 'The Dublin fire brigade 1883-1920' in *Brigade Call,* (Spring 1984), pp 54-7.
[3] Waterworks Committee, *Dublin Corporation annual report, 1891,* vol. iii, pp 251-6.

13

where he was awarded the silver medal of the Royal Society for Preservation of Life from Fire in respect of his work at a fire in Hennessy's Drapers on 19 December 1875. On that occasion Purcell had rescued a woman from the fire and was lowering them both to safety when the rope burned through. They both survived the drop uninjured. At a later stage of his career, when working as an engineer, he had himself lowered into an underground shaft, 95 feet below ground, where a workman had been trapped by a collapse. Purcell worked non-stop for five hours to rescue the man from the mud and water in which he was trapped before allowing himself to be replaced by another volunteer. When he got back to the surface he oversaw the rescue for a further five hours until the workman was successfully removed from the shaft.[4] Thomas Purcell took over as chief officer of the DFB from John Boyle on 14 April 1892. He served until 1917 and made huge changes to the equipment and organisation of the DFB during his years as chief.

Group of firemen at Buckingham Street fire station. *Front row left:* Thomas Smart (senior), coachman/driver at the station. *(Photo: courtesy Colm Smart).*

[4] *The Fireman* magazine, May 1892, p. 210.

Other significant changes were happening in the Brigade at the same time. Dublin firemen, aware of the recommendations of the O`Meara / Harty report which included 'a more elaborate set of rules and regulations detailing the duties of the officers and firemen, and their rigid enforcement'[5] and heading into a new era under a new chief officer, formed a trade union. This union would be the first trade union in a fire service in the British Isles. Many of the members of the DFB had been tradesmen before joining the job and were members of the various unions which represented their callings. Some in fact retained membership of their former trade union in case they left the brigade and returned to their trade. The Dublin Fire Brigademen's Union (DFBU) was formed on 5 June 1892 with a membership of forty-two men. The DFBU affiliated with the Dublin Trades Council and on 24 August 1892 John Simmons, secretary of the trades council submitted a memorial from the men of the DFB from his office at the United Trades Council and Labour League with an address at Trades Hall, Capel Street.[6] In submitting the memorial he also asked the Waterworks committee to receive a deputation from the trades council 'to support the prayer of the memorial'.[7]

The memorial paints a very full picture of the life of a Dublin fireman at this period. It speaks of long hours of duty, poor living conditions, low pay and harsh discipline.[8] A fireman, depending on the duty on which he was rostered, could be on duty for twenty-one or twenty-two hours continuously. Firemen returning to their married quarters after long hours of duty could find themselves unable to go to bed as the rooms were so small (fifteen feet by nine feet) that only one bed would fit in. If it was in use by other family members he would have to wait until another family member got up before he could get some rest.

---

[5]Geraghty and Whitehead, *The Dublin fire brigade,* p. 83.
[6]Dublin Corporation annual report 1892, vol. iii, p. 542.
[7]Reproduced as Appendix C.
[8]Dublin corporation annual report 1892, Vol. iii, pp 541-548.

Firemen on street escape duty suffered great hardship in inclement weather due to a lack of protection from the weather and had no protective clothing of any kind.

The disciplinary procedures were also mentioned. A request that 'when a man is brought before the [Waterworks] Committee for an offence, he shall be allowed to give a personal explanation, and call witnesses in his defence' was included. Other requests were for an extension of daily leave to 11 p.m. and a suggestion that men be allowed go on leave in 'plain clothes' (firemen on joining the service were issued with a uniform and that uniform was to be worn at all times, both on or off duty).

The pay scale was addressed with a request for a first class fireman's rate to be 30s per week with the other grades in proportion. Improvements in the married quarters were requested as were a standardisation of the hours of street escape ladder duty. A request was also made to cease the practice of testing the escape ladders by putting several men on to the ladder. It was pointed out that they could be tested by weight only. No doubt the men were mindful of the fate of Inspector Doherty and Fireman Burke who had died when the overloaded escape ladder broke in Westmoreland Street. A final paragraph appealed for a stop to 'the petty tyranny that we are continually subjected to'. This indicates the level of relations between officers and men within the Brigade at this time. The memorial was signed by forty-two members.

The response of the Waterworks Committee, in a report dated 25 December 1892, was to concede a raise of 1s. 6d. at the starting rate of pay and one shilling per year for each of the following years to a maximum rate of 27s. 6d. after ten years service plus whatever rewards were due from holding a chevron. The hours of leave were extended to 11 o'clock. It was recommended that an arrangement be sanctioned to give the men seven days leave per year and improved accommodation was 'under consideration'.[9]

---

[9]Dublin Corporation annual report, 1892, vol. iii, p. 541-2.

Medal from fire chiefs convention held in Milwaukee, USA, in 1894, presented to Captain Purcell, who attended on behalf of the DFB. *(DFB Museum).*

Prior to this, on 12 November 1892, John Lalor, secretary of the Waterworks Committee, had written to the Trades Council to take issue with the memorial. He pointed out that as far back as 1884 all men dismissed had an opportunity to appear before the committee, some appearing more than once, and some 'whose conduct was too vile' were ordered to be dismissed. An objection raised to the extension of leave from ten to eleven o'clock was that it required the lights to be kept on in the station for an extra hour. The hours of escape duty would not be changed. The men were not used to test the escapes as stated in the memorial but rather to give them confidence in their stability. The Waterworks committee denied that any petty tyranny was practised against the men but, it stated, men must be spoken to and advised for their own good.[10]

[10] *Dublin Corporation annual report 1892,* vol. iii, p. 547-8

Contemporary cartoon of Thomas Purcell.

Three 18th/19th Century fire buckets. The centre one is marked 'REA'
(Royal Exchange Assurance).

Fireman's coat and arm badge and print of the Royal Exchange, the first insurance
company fire brigade set up in Dublin in 1722.

Dublin Fire Brigade brass helmet as worn from 1866-1937.

Fireman's helmet plate from DFB brass helmet.

Chief Officer Thomas
P. Purcell's helmet.

Gilded helmet plate from
Chief Officer Purcell's
helmet. *(Courtesy of DFB
Museum/Purcell family).*

Standard pattern brass helmet as used by Rathmines and Pembroke township brigades.

'Volunteer' pattern helmet worn by many industrial and private fire brigades.

Below: Brass trimmed leather helmet from the Powers Whiskey Distillery fire brigade. This brigade assisted the DFB during Easter Week, 1916.

Above: Standard pattern brass helmet plate.

U.S. Civil War style fireman's 'kepi' worn from 1862-1930.

DFB officer's 'kepi'

Caps were introduced c.1910 for motor drivers to indicate their qualification.

Close up of early cap showing qualification on front.
(Courtsey of Colm Smart)

Fireman's button of the Atlas Assurance Company, which operated a fire engine in Dublin.

Early Dublin Corporation button. Worn by waterworks staff.

Rathmines Fire Brigade brass button.

Dublin Fire Brigade brass button.

Dublin Fire Brigade cap badge
1862-1942.

Pembroke Township fire brigade cap
badge.

Dublin Corporation cap badge worn by
waterworks turncocks attached to the
DFB.

Early DFB badge numbers on cloth
patch to be worn on coat.

Further memorials followed in 1895 and 1898. In 1895 out of a list of improvements sought to pay, leave, accommodation and permission to wear extra clothing at fires in winter to prevent severe wetting, the only improvement granted was an extension to leave to increase it to nine hours per week. In 1898 George Leahy, treasurer of the Dublin Trades Council (DTC) submitted a memorial asking for improvements in daily leave, two weeks annual leave, standard (top) rate of pay for men of seven year's service as opposed to ten years and that married men be allowed the four shillings rent stopped for their rooms.[11] The additional daily leave and the reduction in years of service to obtain full pay were conceded by the Waterworks Committee. In 1898 too, a letter from the DTC includes a copy of a resolution unanimously adopted at their meeting of 29 August 1898 protesting that the conduct of Captain Purcell in ordering the removal of a 1798 commemoration badge from the breast of Fireman Kelly[12] *'was both unjust and arbitrary and calculated to hamper the liberty,*

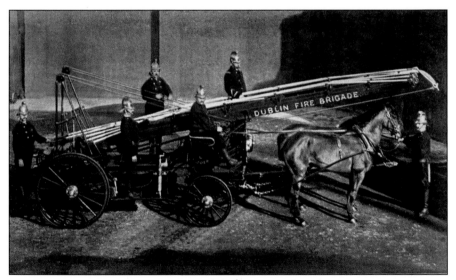

One of Purcell's horse drawn extension ladders. *(Courtesy of Purcell family).*

[11] *Dublin Corporation minutes 1898,* pp 333-4.
[12] There are two Kellys listed on the brigades strength at this time, badge no. 34, Matthew Kelly and badge no. 43, Christopher Kelly. It is not known to which of these men this letter refers.

both civic and political of the body over which he had control . . . and that in the interests of individual liberty and as an endeavour to counteract petty tyranny that a copy of this resolution be sent to the town clerk'.[13] There is further evidence of friction between Purcell and the members of the union but it is important to state that little survives by way of documentation from the early years of the DFB, mainly due to the actions of Major J.J Comerford when chief officer of the brigade after his appointment in 1938. Major Comerford asked for and was given permission to destroy records over seven years old.[14] Thus, much of the early written records of the DFB were lost to waste paper drives in the years of the Emergency and this destruction of old records was a regular feature of Brigade life for many years.

Belfast Fire Brigade ambulance. Purcell saw this vehicle while on a visit to Belfast in 1897 and instituted a similar service in Dublin the following year
(Liam O`Luanaigh collection).

[13]*Dublin Corporation minutes 1898,* pp 245-6.

[14]Geraghty and Whitehead, *Dublin fire brigade,* p. 218.

Purcell, while he does not seem sympathetic to the memorials of the Trades Council, was a far seeing officer whose technical genius is unchallenged. He designed and put into service a horse drawn 66ft extension ladder. This could be extended to 100ft by the use of additional separate ladders and was a forerunner of the modern turntable ladder. He travelled widely to study firefighting techniques in Europe and the United States and introduced many innovations to Dublin. The stations he designed and put in place in Buckingham Street (1901), Dorset Street (1902), Tara Street (1907) and Thomas Street (1913) served the city for many years. Following a visit to Belfast Fire Brigade in 1897 where he saw that brigade's horse drawn ambulance in use he had designed a similar but improved vehicle for the DFB and instituted the brigade's ambulance service in 1898. This replaced the previous ambulance service which had been provided by the Dublin Metropolitan Police for a number of years. He is remembered as the man who designed the first motor fire engine for Dublin in 1909. His was a professional brigade which served the city well. Whether the firemen were as well served by their employers is a different question.

Architect's drawing of Thomas Street station *(Courtesy of DFB Museum)*.

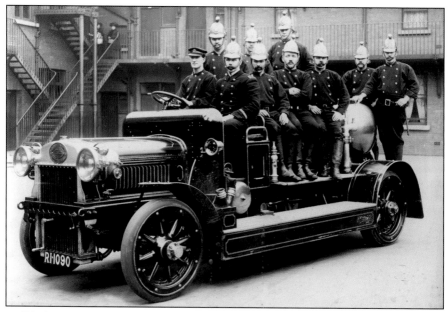

RI 1090, the brigade's first motor fire engine, in Tara Street fire station. Built to Purcell's design by Leyland Motors in 1909 *(Photo: DFB Museum collection)*.

The start of the new century dawned and in March of 1900 the Waterworks Committee reviewed a memorial from the DTC on behalf of Dublin firemen seeking improvements in leave and pay.[15] The pay claim was based on increased duties, partly due to the introduction of the Brigade's ambulance service in 1898. Purcell reviewed the memorial and passed his comments on to the chairman and members of the Waterworks Committee in a letter in which he refers to the previous memorials of 1892, 1895 and 1898. He remarks negatively on each of the points raised in the latest memorial and points out that if his reorganisation scheme for the Brigade is carried out 'night duty on the streets would be done away with, the brigade better distributed and housed, night duty in stations modified and periods of leave put on a more regular and equitable basis'. The memorial was turned down. A second one was sent which restated the claims. It too was turned down by the committee.[16]

[15] *Dublin Corporation annual report, 1900,* vol. i, pp 467-80.
[16] *Dublin Corporation annual report, 1900,* vol. ii, pp 649-53.

An indication of the state of industrial relations within the Brigade comes from a letter held in the DFB museum dated 16 February 1906. The letter, addressed to 'Dear O'Hara' and written by E.L Richardson[18] is intriguing as it presents one side of an argument. It informs O'Hara of an apology from the Captain to 'Giffney and the men'. While the letter indicates a matter of some gravity in which the Captain 'faced public censure if not dismissal', it carries no details of the incident to which it refers. Its value lies in the insight it offers to the relationship between the chief and at least some of his firemen. E.L Richardson is also the author of a letter from the DTC to the Waterworks Committee in 1907 seeking a raise of 2s 6d per week and making the point that the extension of the city boundaries, the opening of the new stations and the development of the ambulance service had resulted in more exacting duties.[19] The increase was sanctioned by the Waterworks Committee in spite of objections from Captain Purcell.

The Dublin Fire Brigademen's Union (DFBU) first made a return to the Registrar of Friendly Societies in December 1912. From this point on it functioned as a trade union in its own right and pursued matters in its own name rather than under the umbrella of the Dublin Trades Council. The secretary was P.T. Daly and the treasurer was Fireman Joseph Lynch.[20]

As a public service trade union, the DFBU was not involved in the Dublin lockout of 1913. The firemen made their sympathies known however. Collections were made for the strike fund and regular donations were made to the locked out workers. The DMP regarded the firemen as on the side of their locked out fellow trade unionists. David Nelligan, speaking of his time as a young constable in the DMP, remarked that: *'the Dublin Fire Brigade also was unfriendly to the police, they too were on the radical side and always surly to the force'*.[21]

---

[17]DFB Museum collection, accession no. 033/08 (reproduced as appendix F).
[18]Secretary of the Irish Trade Union Congress (ITUC).
[19]*Dublin Corporation annual report 1907*, vol. ii, pp 905-11.
[20]P.T Daly was also secretary of the DTUC and the ITUC.
  Later he was one of the committee which formed the Irish Citizen Army.
[21]Nelligan, *The spy in the castle*, pp 51-2.

The DFB annual report for 1913 comments that owing to abnormal labour disturbances in the city and surrounding county during the latter months of the year incendiarism was very prevalent, particularly in farm produce. In Purcell's handwritten notes for the report his comments are more caustic; '10 incendiary fires in county' - "Larkinism".[22]

Foreman Mick Fox and Fireman Tom Morris with their sons at Thomas Street fire station *c* 1914. *(Courtesy of the Fox family).*

[22]DFB Museum collection, Purcell papers.

CHAPTER 3

War and rebellion: 1914-1916

THE Dublin lockout ended officially on 18 January 1914 with what many would regard as a Pyrrhic victory for the Dublin employers. A by product of the lockout had been the formation of a workers militia, the Irish Citizen Army (ICA). Although formed initially to protect union meetings and to defend the striking workers against attacks from the police and strike breakers, it was maintained after the lockout to provide a military force to take part in armed rebellion against British rule in Ireland. It was the belief of union leader and socialist James Connolly that armed conflict was inevitable and that the ICA would be a part of it. It was his belief that the ICA, with or without the assistance of the Volunteer movement, should stage an uprising during the course of the forthcoming European war which was seen as inevitable. Writing in the *Irish Worker* in 1914 he stated 'The Citizen Army Offices at Liberty Hall, Aungier Street, Inchicore, Thomas Street, and elsewhere are open every night for enrollment. We want a new muster of men prepared to face the worst and to take the best if taken it can be.'[1]

The events in the Balkans following the assassination of Austria's Archduke Franz Ferdinand and Germany's declaration of war on Russia, followed by the German invasion of Belgium, meant that Great Britain and France, bound by treaty obligations, declared war on Germany. War was declared on 4 August 1914. The declaration of war was soon followed by a major recruiting campaign for the British armed forces across the whole United Kingdom of Great Britain and Ireland. Public euphoria and support for the war by politicians of both nationalist and unionist

---

[1] *Irish Worker,* 24 October 1914.

persuasions led many Irishmen to enlist. It can be argued that economic conditions in Dublin in the aftermath of the lockout led many unemployed men to the recruiting sergeants but there was genuine support for the war across many, if not all, economic and political classes. The Irish National Volunteers, formed in 1913, split, with most of the members supporting the calls of Irish Party leader John Redmond to enlist and fight for the freedom of small nations. The remaining members, now reconstituted as the Irish Volunteers, and with key positions in the organisation held by members of the Irish Republican Brotherhood, began to arm and train for an uprising.

Recruiting for the British Army continued and two members of the DFB enlisted. Due to the loss of early records already referred to, little is known of the prewar service of Fireman John Murphy. He is referred to in the DFB annual report for 1915 as 'Corporal Murphy, A.S.C, serving with the Mediterranean Expeditionary Force'.[2] He survived the war and returned to the brigade in 1919.

Recent research[3] has thrown much more light on the other recruit from the DFB, Fireman Patrick Bruton. Born in Milltown, Co. Meath, Patrick gave his age as thirty-four years on enlistment. He joined the 1st Battalion Irish Guards on 5 September 1914. He was promoted to lance corporal on 1 January 1915 and lance sergeant (a rank peculiar to the Guards regiments of the British army) on 22 April 1915. Wounded at the battle of Loos in 1915 he recuperated in hospital in England before returning to the western front where he earned a Military Medal (M.M.), awarded on 29 November 1916. Following a further wound he again spent time in hospital in England before returning to the regiment and was discharged on 19 April 1919.[4] The 1911 census shows 'firebrigade man' Patrick Bruton, born Co. Meath, living in Buckingham Street Dublin. This is the same address given in the attestation papers in 1914 and is

[2]Army Service Corps.

[3]*Firecall magazine,* Two part article 'From Buckingham street to the western front' Autumn and Winter editions 2011.

[4]Attestation papers and service record of no. 5115, Patrick Bruton, Irish Guards Regimental Museum, Birdcage Walk, London. Bruton / Houghton family.

presumably Buckingham Street fire station. However, Patrick's age is given in the 1911 census as thirty-five years old, making him thirty-eight in 1914. It would appear that Patrick falsified his age to make himself appear younger and able for service with an elite infantry regiment. His motives, be they loyalty or a sense of adventure, are lost to history but it is interesting that his brother Martin had also served the state as a member of the DMP (warrant no.10176) from 1898 to 1905 prior to emigrating to Canada to pursue a career in the police there.[5]

Fireman Patrick Bruton, DFB. *(Photo: author's collection).*

[5]DMP personnel register, Garda Museum, Dublin Castle.

Recruiting figures for DFB members can be compared with those for both Belfast fire brigade and Cork City fire brigade. In 1914 Belfast had six men who were reservists with either the Royal Navy or the army and who were recalled to the colours on the outbreak of war. A further twenty men volunteered for service by December 1914.[6] The establishment of the Belfast fire brigade at that period was just under seventy men so it can be seen that over one third of the brigade enlisted which caused major manpower shortages. This required the transfer to the brigade of ten members of the Royal Irish Constabulary as temporary firemen while others were recruited to make up the shortfall.

At least three men enlisted from Cork City fire brigade which numbered twenty men, eight of whom were full time with the others acting as auxiliaries as required. One of these, Fireman John Keating, was killed in action at Mons in 1914 while serving with the Royal Munster Fusiliers which suggests that he was a reservist rather than a new recruit. Two other firemen are listed as serving in a Cork Examiner article and the position of six others is unclear as their fire brigade positions (if any) are not given. The article names twenty four men with service in Cork fire brigade or family connections to the brigade who were serving at the time, 'a record unequalled in any other brigade in the kingdom'.[7]

The enlistment of only two men from the Dublin Fire Brigade in spite of a decision by Dublin Corporation and other public bodies to keep the jobs open and to continue to pay half the wages of any workmen, including firemen, who enlisted is interesting. If the heavy recruiting from Belfast can be seen as a political statement from an overwhelmingly Unionist brigade, the lack of support for recruiting from the DFB's ranks may perhaps be seen as support for the labour / nationalist anti- recruiting position.

[6]William Broadhurst and Henry Walsh, *The flaming truth: a history of the Belfast fire Brigade* (Belfast, 2001), pp. 145-7.
[7]*Cork Examiner,* 6 January 1916.

In Dublin, life continued as normal for the brigade. Some additional duties were caused by the war including regular attendance by the brigade's ambulances (and those of the township brigades) at the North Wall to help unload the hospital ships bringing wounded soldiers from the base hospitals in France. Both the existing King George V military hospital and the new military hospital in Dublin Castle dealt with the casualties and many private homes and 'big houses' operated as convalescent homes for wounded soldiers. An addition to the brigade's fleet was the 'cinema ambulance' purchased by the cinema owners of Dublin and built to Captain Purcell's specifications. The cinema ambulance was to be used primarily for the removal of wounded troops but could also be used as part of the Brigade's ambulance fleet when not required for its main purpose.[8]

In late 1915 a new recruit joined Dublin Fire Brigade as a probationary fireman.[9] Born in 1893, Joseph (Joe) Connolly was the grandson of a family evicted during the land war of the 1880s from a small farm near Straffan, Co. Kildare and he and his family were heavily involved in both socialist and nationalist politics.[10] His father Michael had been at sea and following his return to Dublin he took up a post as a swing bridge operator on Dublin's docks and moved his family to 58 Lower Gloucester Street. In the 1911 census Michael Connolly is listed as a dock porter and Joseph as a messenger. Michael and his sons, John, Joseph, George, Matthew and Edward could all read and write and had both Irish and English. Joseph's older brother John, or Sean as he was known, was a clerk with Dublin Corporation motor licence department located at City Hall. All the brothers, as well as their sister Kathleen (Katie) Barrett were members of the Irish Citizen Army. Joe Connolly had joined the ICA in 1915 and was a member when he joined the DFB.

On Easter Monday 1916, units of the Irish Citizen Army and the Irish Volunteers took over positions in Dublin city and declared a republic.

---

[8] Geraghty and Whitehead, *The Dublin fire brigade,* p.148.

[9] First appears in the accounts book of the DFBU in December 1915, DFBU accounts book, DFB Museum.

[10] Connolly, Mike, Johannesburg, South Africa, Email, 23 September 2008.

This was the rebellion for which they had planned and it was launched in spite of a countermanding order from Eoin MacNeill, the leader of the Volunteers who realised that the IRB elements within the Volunteers planned military action which he felt had no hope of success. Under the Military Council, which included Patrick Pearse and James Connolly, the Rising went ahead and depleted units of the Volunteers and ICA seized buildings in Dublin city centre.

One of the small bands of insurgents which went out that morning was tasked with attacking Dublin Castle and holding buildings in the vicinity to control access to the castle. It was led by Captain Sean Connolly and included his brothers George, Matthew, Edward and sister Katie. They marched off from Liberty Hall, the ICA's headquarters, across Butt Bridge and came up Tara Street where they stopped at the fire station. Sean Connolly sent for Joe, who was on duty, and told him to report to Liberty Hall where he was required. Joe Connolly was a driver with the brigade at a time when driving motor vehicles was a rare accomplishment. In his unpublished account of the rising, Matt Connolly described the scene:

> *We moved sharply across Butt Bridge along Tara Street, past the fire*
> *station where Joe, another brother, who was a member of the Dublin*
> *Fire Brigade had a few hurried words with Sean as we passed by.*
> *It was later learned that Sean had told Joe to report at once*
> *to Commandant Connolly at Liberty Hall where there was a*
> *special job for him as one of the very few motor drivers in*
> *the organisation Joe changed out of DFB uniform and left*
> *the station.*[11]

This account is also borne out by the Bureau of Military History (BMH) witness statements of William Oman[12] and Rose Hackett.[13] According to family history he commandeered a car at Butt bridge and drove it to Liberty Hall. He loaded arms and equipment there and delivered them

---

[11]Matt Connolly's eye witness account, unpublished manuscript, Connolly family papers.
[12]William Oman, Bureau of Military History witness statement, Military Archives,
  Cathal Brugha Barracks, Dublin, W.S. 421, p. 5.
[13]Rose Hackett, BMH witness statement W.S. 546, p. 5.

to the rebel headquarters at the GPO and is included on a list of the garrison there on the first day of the rising.[14] He left the GPO and reported to the ICA garrison at St. Stephens Green / College of Surgeons where he served for the rest of the week under Michael Mallin and Countess de Markievicz. He was on the roof of the College of Surgeons and was heavily involved in counter sniping at British troops.[15] He is also mentioned as rescuing a wounded comrade under machine gun fire.[16] Joe was unhappy with the order to surrender at the end of Easter week and produced an automatic pistol to shoot the British officer who came to take the surrender but was overpowered by other volunteers.[17]

After the surrender Joe and the other members of the garrison were marched to Richmond Barracks in Inchicore. Here detectives from the 'G' division of the DMP moved among them spotting officers and other leaders of the rebellion. One of the detectives, Johnny Barton, stopped in front of Joe Connolly and asked his name although, as a political detective, he knew Joe on sight. When Connolly answered, Barton said;

> *'Sean is dead', Joe replied 'He died for his country'. To which Barton retorted 'He was a disgrace to his country'. Joe replied, 'That is what you say. I am proud of him. He's a better Irishman than you will ever be'.*[18]

Sean Connolly had been killed at City Hall in the first hours of the rising. On arrival at the gates of Dublin Castle he had shot the policeman on duty, Constable James O'Brien, when he attempted to shut the castle gate. Sean's unit took up positions in the area and he entered Dublin City Hall (to which he had keys as a corporation employee based there). His unit was engaged by British troops firing from Dublin Castle and Sean was shot and killed on the roof of City Hall by a sniper. He had inflicted the first Crown Force's fatality of the Rising and became the first republican fatality.

---

[14] R.M. Fox, *The history of the Irish Citizen Army* (Dublin, 1944), p. 227.

[15] James O'Shea, BMH witness statement W.S 733, pp 48, 50.

[16] James O'Shea, BMH witness statement W.S. 733, p. 50.

[17] William Oman, BMH witness statement W.S. 421, p. 12.

[18] Frank Robbins, *Under the starry plough: recollections of the Irish Citizen Army* (Dublin, 1977), p. 130.

Sean Connolly's memorial card. *(Connolly family papers).*

Among a group of 197 prisoners listed for deportation to Wandsworth Prison on 9 May 1916 is 'Joseph Connolly, Fire Station, Tara Street, Dublin.'[19] He was released on 17 July 1916 and returned to duty with Dublin Fire Brigade. His return was facilitated by the regulations put in place to allow corporation workmen who enlisted in the British army return to the corporation when hostilities ended.

The week of the Easter Rising was the busiest in the Brigade's history up to that point. The first call came to the control room in Tara Street at 3.58pm on 24 April when a call was received from the Ordnance Department, Islandbridge, to a fire in the magazine fort, Phoenix Park. This incident was to be the cause of controversy and to bring about a public disagreement between Captain Purcell and Lieutenant John Myers, the DFB second in command. The call was sent to 'A' station (Thomas Street) who responded via Steevens Lane and Kingsbridge. A second section of the brigade was sent from 'B' station (Tara Street) under

---

[19] *1916 Rebellion handbook* (Dublin, 1998), p. 79.

the command of Lieutenant Myers. In Captain Purcell's account for the *Irish Times Rebellion Handbook* he stated that this section was held up by 'Sinn Feiners' at a barricade and that a loaded revolver was placed at the driver's head and the section was ordered to return.[20] *The Irish Times* on 5 May stated that 'Lieutenant Myers, of the Dublin Fire Brigade, requests us to contradict the statement, in a recent issue, that he was held up at a barricade by Sinn Féiners with loaded revolvers while proceeding to the fire at the Magazine in the Phoenix Park'.

Apart from the Magazine fort, the first two major fires fought by the DFB on the first day of the Rising were in shoe shops, the Cable Shoe Company and the True Form shoe shop, both in Sackville Street, which were looted and burned.[21] Dublin's barefoot poor were taking advantage of the rebellion. Looting of shops, which were then set on fire, was a feature of the early days of the fighting and both the fire and ambulance services of the brigade were at full stretch. The brigade ambulances were augmented by Red Cross ambulances manned by volunteer crews and the numerous St. John's Ambulance Brigade Voluntary Aid Detachments (VADs) which were a feature of many business houses in the city in those days. All worked under fire at times and Corps Superintendent Holden Stoddart of the St. John's ambulance was shot dead in the Baggot St. area.[22] No DFB firemen were killed but a number of civilians were shot dead in close proximity to firemen in the Sackville Street area and Captain Purcell was forced to order the men to abandon equipment and leave the danger zone.

The centre of the city burned as shops and other premises caught fire from adjoining premises, were deliberately set on fire by looters, or as a result of shelling by the military. In a number of cases the firemen were forced to rescue over-enthusiastic looters who had become trapped by the fires which they themselves had started. By Thursday 27 April there was a major conflagration in the centre of Dublin which lit up the night sky

[20] *Rebellion handbook,* pp 29-30.
[21] *Rebellion handbook,* p. 30.
[22] *Rebellion handbook,* p. 232.

and could be seen for many miles outside the city. The firemen were working around the clock with only short breaks for sleep and meals. Due to the fact that they could not get to many fires in the areas where military action was heaviest, they were fighting a losing battle. In the townships the local Brigades were fully involved in dealing with the results of fighting in their own area and were unable to assist the city Brigade. Major fires were burning in the Sackville Street area and in the Abbey Street / Henry Street areas. On the afternoon of 27 April the fires started to join up in what Purcell referred to as 'the Great Fire'. The fires spread rapidly and soon entire blocks were burning. By Saturday 30 April the Brigade was working with firefighters from both the Guinness Brewery Fire Brigade and the Brigade from Power's Distillery in Thomas Street to save Jervis Street hospital from the surrounding flames. After the surrender the Brigade could concentrate its resources and by Sunday morning the main fires were under control.

Firemen in the ruins of Abbey Street, Easter 1916.
(Photo courtesy of National Library of Ireland).

R.I.C. depot, Phoenix Park, 1903. Police recruits receive firefighting training.
See Appendix B. (*Courtesy Police Museum, Belfast. RUC G.C. Historical Society*).

Page from Shand Mason catalogue. Public or private fire brigades could order their equipment from this and similar catalogues. *(Courtesy of Niall Tier).*

Kingstown (Dun Laoghaire) hose tender 1902. *(Courtesy of Liam O Luanaigh).*

Dublin Fire Brigade hose tender c1900. Note 'City Fire Brigade' letting on this vehicle. *(Courtesy Eamonn Moran).*

E. & S., Ltd., D.]   **Military Operations, Dublin, June-July, 1922.**   [Photo, Hogan, I
NATIONAL FORCES BOMBING HAMMAM HOTEL.

Dublin and Rathmines Fire Brigades in Michael Collins' funeral procession. First in line is the Tara Street section, driven by Thomas Smart, followed by the Thomas Street section driven by Bernard Matthews and the last vehicle is the Rathmines Fire Brigade driven by James Heather-Thomas. (*Courtesy of the National Library of Ireland*).

Collins funeral: Dublin Fire Brigade Thomas Street section and Rathmines Fire Brigade.
(Courtesy of the National Library of Ireland).

Firemen pose on armoured car. *(Courtesy of Janice Broe).*

Minature versions of Thomas Smart's 1916 and War of Independence medals.
(Courtesy Colm Smart).

Horse drawn Shand Mason steamer at Buckingham Street fire station c1900.
(Courtesy of Colm Smart).

Military cordon at Custom House *(South Dublin Libraries Collection).*

The Brigade was praised on all sides. The British trade magazine *'Fire'* remarked that 'the troubled days of the week-end rebellion proved how nobly Irish firemen, and more particularly Dublin and Pembroke firemen, answered the call to them as warriors of peace'.[23] The damage to buildings alone was estimated by Purcell at two and a half million pounds.[24]

The surrender of the Volunteer and ICA garrisons was a bitter disappointment to many of the men who had fought but so too was the reaction of many ordinary Dubliners. Prisoners being marched to detention and trial, under military escort, were jeered and abused by many Dublin citizens. While this was the common experience of many volunteers one man had a different memory. Joseph Good was a member of the Kimmage garrison. He had fought in the G.P.O. and was one of the volunteers held overnight at the Rotunda after the surrender;

> *From the Rotunda we marched along O`Connell Street. A solitary*
> *fireman was working near Kelly's corner and he said out loud;*
> *'I'm with you boys'. That was the first word of approval I had*
> *heard from Dubliners that week.*[25]

The aftermath of the rising brought some recognition of the efforts of the men of the DFB. In Royal Barracks, Dublin on 27 May 1916, General John Maxwell inspected ambulances used during the Rising. Among the ambulance crews attending was a DFB ambulance with three Dublin firemen, John O'Connor, John Williams and Joseph Lynch. Sir John Maxwell, in a brief address, said the military in Dublin were deeply thankful for the work done by the ambulances.[26] A more concrete gesture was the decision made by the Dublin Corporation to grant a chevron carrying a one shilling pay rise to each man who was on duty through that week. The corporation also voted a bonus of £50 to both Captain Purcell and Lieutenant Myers in recognition of their efforts during the rising.[27]

[23] *Fire* magazine, June 1916.
[24] Purcell family papers.
[25] Joseph Good, BMH witness statement, W.S. 388, pp 19-20.
[26] *Rebellion handbook,* p. 107.
[27] *Dublin corporation annual report 1916,* vol ii, pp 417-9.

Captain Purcell was also awarded the bronze medal of the British Fire Prevention Committee 'as a token of regard for the splendid work done by him and his brigade during most trying circumstances during the Irish Rebellion of 1916'.[28]

The events of the rising had an echo later that year when Fireman Joe Connolly returned to the brigade. He was reinstated and made permanent.[29] Later that year he applied for, and was paid 'wages which accrued due amounting to £22 10s. 0d., during absence from the brigade, he having been deported in connection with the disturbance during Easter Week'.[30]

[28]Geraghty and Whitehead, *The Dublin Fire Brigade,* p. 154.
[29]*Dublin corporation annual report 1917,* vol i, p. 319.
[30]*Dublin corporation annual report 1917,* vol i, p. 692.

CHAPTER 4

Revolution 1917-1921

CAPTAIN Purcell was badly injured in an accident on 16 November 1916 when he was thrown from his horse drawn trap while responding to a fire in Suffolk Street. He was on sick leave for a period and made application to the Waterworks Committee for permission to retire on 16 October 1917. His request was accepted at the November meeting of the committee and Thomas Purcell retired leaving behind him a Brigade vastly different to that which he had inherited from John Boyle in 1892. To the end he was a diligent servant of the Corporation and a sharp observer of life in the city. In his notes for his final annual report in 1917, his 'twenty sixth, last and valedictory report', he notes a fire at Alexandra Road Wharf involving fodder for the British War Department which cost a £14,500 loss. He states in his handwritten notes that *the fire was caused by spontaneous combustion of damp fermenting hay in centre of bales, shoved in by sellers to make good paying weight for the blundering War Department*. The fact that it was recorded as a malicious claim and had to be paid by the city was in his verdict, delivered in capital letters, 'DAMNABLE'.[1]

He was replaced as Chief Officer by his lieutenant, John Myers, who had served in the Brigade since 1897.

A number of incidents occurred around this time which point to a new influence within the Brigade. A recruiting banner had been fixed to the G.P.O. by the British military authorities. It had a picture of Lord Kitchener and carried a recruiting message for the British Army. The canvas streamer was a major irritant to the Volunteers, and Volunteer Sean Harling was ordered to destroy it. He lit the banner by throwing a

[1] Thomas Purcell, personal papers

paraffin soaked sod of turf into it. The banner blazed and soon the fire brigade was called. Sean Harling, recalling the event for Kenneth Griffiths book, *Curious Journey*, describes how 'the fire brigade came along then. Joe Connolly, whose brother Sean was killed in 1916, was one of them. Well they looked and saw what was burning and turned around and went back.'[2]

On the final day of September 1917 the Dublin Fire Brigade took part in the biggest nationalist demonstration held in the city since the Rising. Thomas Ashe, a hero of the 1916 Rising had died from complications caused by forced feeding while on hunger strike. The event was stage managed as a show of strength by the Volunteers and for the first time since the Rising, armed and uniformed Volunteers paraded on the streets of the capital. Ashe's body lay in state in the City Hall watched over by an honour guard of Volunteers and the funeral itself was a massive occasion. Members of the Volunteers, the Fianna and Cumann na mBan marched, as did contingents from many public bodies, trade unions and other organisations. One of the organisations which took part was the Dublin Fire Brigade. The brigade attended with two motor engines under the command of Lieutenant Myers and two horse drawn wagons followed by a trap with Captain Purcell and driven by a fireman.[3]

The most unusual thing about the DFB contingent was noted by Douglas Goldring, an English journalist . . . *'the Dublin Fire Brigade went clanking by on their engines, the men in full uniform with shining brass helmets and all of them wearing Sinn Fein armlets'.*[4] *When he commented on the armlets to a bystander he was told 'sure aren't they Irishmen too?'*

In a separate incident a DFB ambulance was called to the North Wall in the port of Dublin where a grain ship had docked. The *SS War Cypress* was on her maiden voyage and carrying grain loaded in New Orleans. The normal procedure would have been for the ship to open the covers of the hold prior to berthing in order to allow any build up of fumes or gas to

[2] Kenneth Griffiths and Timothy O'Grady, *Curious Journey* (Dublin, 1998), pp 97-8.
[3] *Freemans Journal*, 1 October, 1917.
[4] Glenn Hooper, *The tourist's gaze*, (Cork, 2001) p.173.

disperse. This was not done and when the casual labourers being employed to unload the cargo entered the hold they were overcome by gas as were others on the deck. When the DFB ambulance arrived with Firemen Joseph Lynch and Edward (Ned) Doyle, they attempted to enter the hold and Lynch was overcome. Ned Doyle went down into the hold and tied lines to each of the men. Lynch recovered consciousness and the men were removed from the hold. Four men were found to be dead on arrival at the hospital and, but for the actions of Doyle, the toll would have been higher. While such an action would normally merit the award of a chevron for lifesaving it appears that the Waterworks Committee were not in favour of such an award as the DFB men were already on a wartime bonus for additional cost of living expenses associated with the war and it was felt that additional payments would be a drain on the taxpayers of Dublin. The coroner recommended a monetary award for the firemen. In fact the men were awarded £10 and a citation from the Carnegie Heroes Fund, £10 from the Admiralty Fund, A Royal Humane Society bronze medal and for the first time in the DFB, they were awarded the King's Police and Fire Medal.[5] The King's Police and Fire Medal, usually shortened to King's Police Medal or K.P.M, was a very prestigious award on a par with the Victoria Cross.

The medal was presented at Buckingham Palace by the king himself or in the case of Irish awards, by the Lord Lieutenant in a ceremony at the RIC Depot in the Phoenix Park (Irish recipients would tend to be members of the RIC or DMP). This was a rare and major award. The award of the K.P.M. to the two firemen was announced in the Irish Times and the ceremony was arranged for 2 July 1919.[6] While Fireman Doyle accepted the medal, Joseph Lynch, in an unprecedented move, refused the award in April 1919.[7] After the ceremony the medal was returned, unissued, to the Home Office. Joseph Lynch did not state a reason for his

[5] *DFB annual report,* 1918, pp 10-11.
[6] *Irish Times,* 1 January, 1919.
[7] Edward Doyle's Royal Humane Society medal and K.P.M in family possession.

refusal of the K.P.M. but he did accept the other awards which suggests that it may have been politically motivated. Lynch had been a stalwart member of the Dublin Fire Brigademen's Union which he had served as treasurer and in a number of other posts.

Fireman Edward Doyle *c.*1918 *(Courtesy of the Doyle family)*.

On the political front this was a period of reorganisation and rearming for the Volunteers, now known as the Irish Republican Army. While many members of the ICA had realigned themselves with IRA units after the rising, the ICA itself still existed as a separate body and Joe Connolly remained a member. Both bodies cooperated, especially in the importation of arms where the ICA's links to the Dublin dockworkers was a major benefit. The IRA order of battle in Dublin at this period was based on four battalions. These were: 1st Battalion in the northwest of the city, 2nd Battalion in the north east, 3rd Battalion in the south east and 4th Battalion in the south west. The Liffey was the dividing line between battalion areas north and south. There was a 5th Battalion which was composed of engineers which dealt with explosives, communications etc. Its members were spread among the other battalions to form the engineer element in each one. These units formed the IRA's 'Dublin Brigade'. At all levels from brigade down to local company the value of intelligence work was emphasised. Intelligence officers and staff gathered all available information and established a network of agents and sympathisers at all levels in society. Without doubt the value of contacts within the Dublin Fire Brigade would have been recognised and encouraged. The IRA had agents within the RIC and DMP even to the extent of infiltrating the DMP's G division, the political detectives who would be their main adversaries in the early stages of the coming war. The IRA also formed units to carry the fight forward. Along with each individual company and battalion, the brigade itself formed an 'Active Service Unit' or ASU. The director of Intelligence, Michael Collins, formed a group of counter intelligence officers known as 'the Squad'[8] to collate intelligence and take direct action against any threat to the republican movement.

The storm broke not in Dublin, but on a quiet road in Tipperary on 21 January 1919. On the day that Dáil Éireann met in the Mansion House in Dublin to establish a Provisional Government of the Irish Republic, volunteers from the South Tipperary brigade of the IRA ambushed two RIC constables escorting a cart load of dynamite to a quarry near Soloheadbeg. Constable James McDonnell, fifty-seven years old with thirty-six years police service and Constable Patrick O'Connell, thirty-six years old with twelve years service in the RIC, were shot dead by the IRA party.[9] More policemen were to die that spring and summer in Limerick city and county and in Tipperary but it was only after a visit to the DMP detective unit headquarters in Brunswick Street (when he was smuggled in by a contact within the police) that Collins decided to move against the G division detectives.[10]

---

[8] T. Ryle Dwyer, *The Squad* (Cork, 2005), pp 52-3.
[9] Richard Abbott, *Police casualties in Ireland 1919-1922* (Cork, 2000), pp 30-3.
[10] Michael T. Foy, *Michael Collins's intelligence war* (Stroud, 2006), p. 21.

The first detective to be shot in Dublin was Detective Sergeant Patrick Smyth. He was making his way home to his house in Drumcondra on 30 July 1919 when he was attacked and shot by five gunmen.[11] Smyth actually survived the initial attack and asked his son to call the ambulance. Joe Lawless, a member of the squad, who had not taken part in the shooting but lived nearby, kept an eye on proceedings;

> *a few inquisitive people began to drift towards the scene of the shooting and about twenty minutes later the Dublin Fire Brigade ambulance went clattering over the bridge. I walked down myself then, as quite a crowd had collected there and was just in time to see sergeant Smyth being carried from his house to the ambulance. Joe Connolly, the ambulance driver whom I knew as a Volunteer, remarked to me, rather disappointedly, I thought, 'I don't think he is dead yet'.*[12]

Smyth died in the Mater Hospital on 11 September 1919 as a result of the wounds received in the shooting. One result of this shooting was a refinement of tactics used by the squads gunmen. They had shot Smyth with .38 calibre revolvers which did not inflict the same damage as the larger .45 calibre revolvers they favoured afterward. The fact that he had been able to run towards his home after being shot was also addressed. In future the preferred tactic was for an initial shot to the body to knock the victim down followed by a *coup de grace* to the head.

Smyth was the first of the G men to be killed but others followed including Johnny Barton who had confronted Joe Connolly in Richmond barracks in 1916. He was shot dead in College Street, Dublin on 29 November 1919.[13] The effect of these assassinations was to blunt the edge of British intelligence on the republican movement. As the war intensified, in the south and west of the country especially, Dublin became the scene of regular street shootings and ambushes.

[11] Abbott, *Police casualties,* pp 40-2.
[12] Michael T. Foy, *Michaels Collins's intelligence war,* p. 25.
[13] Abbott, *Police casualties,* pp 46-7.

Dublin firemen achieved an important victory in their struggle for better conditions when, in January 1920, the Waterworks Committee sanctioned a change in working conditions to allow every third day off following two full days on duty (forty eight hours on, twenty four off). However a dispute arose because of differing interpretations of the new system and it looked briefly that the DFB might be entering its first industrial dispute.[14] At this time also there was a move away from the DFBU by some firemen and a number of other unions began to represent firemen. DFB membership was now divided between the DFBU, the Irish Transport and General Workers Union, the Building Labourers Union and the Irish Municipal Employees Trade Union with some of officer rank represented by the Local Government Officers [Ireland] Trade Union.

In view of the new working hours more firemen were needed and among the recruits to the DFB who joined in this period were Michael Rogers, Austin McDonald and Thomas Smart.

Michael Joseph Rogers was born on 6 April 1896 in Dublin and worked as a tram driver before joining the DFB on 27 September 1918. Austin McDonald was born on 20 August 1897 in Louisburgh, Co. Mayo and worked as a shop assistant before joining the DFB on 26 January 1920. Thomas Smart, a motor driver and the son of a fireman, was born in Dublin on 25 September 1896 and also joined the DFB on 26 January 1920.[15] Each of these men was starting a new career in the DFB. Each had something else in common. They were members of the Irish Republican Army.

Thomas Smart had been in the Volunteers since 1915. He was the son of Fireman Thomas Smart of Buckingham Street fire station and is listed in the 1911 census as a fourteen year old messenger. At that time he was living in married quarters in Buckingham Street fire station with his parents, three brothers and three sisters. By 1915 he was working in Becker Brothers, tea merchants, and joined 'C' company of the volunteers

---

[14]Geraghty and Whitehead, *Dublin fire brigade,* pp 161-3.
[15]DFB personnel records, DFB Museum collection.

Thomas Smart in volunteer uniform. *(Photo courtesy Colm Smart)*.

1st battalion at their headquarters, no. 41 Parnell Square. On Easter Monday his unit was assigned to the Four Courts garrison and he saw heavy action in the Four Courts and Church Street areas during the week of the Rising.[16] On Wednesday, 26 April, in order to remove the threat to the garrison from soldiers of the Royal Dublin Fusiliers firing from vantage points in the buildings on the corner of Bridge Street and Ushers Quay, Tom Smart, with Peadar Clancy crossed Church Street Bridge under intense rifle fire.[17] The men forced an entry to the building being used as a strongpoint by the military and set fire to the ground floor. They then withdrew to the Four Courts by recrossing the bridge, again under concentrated fire. The fire they started denied the use of the building to the British military and in fact grew into a serious fire that was noted on Captain Purcell's map of fires in the city caused by the Rising. After the surrender order was given to the men of this garrison it was made clear that anyone not in uniform who had the chance to escape should take it.

---

[16]Thomas Smart, BMH WS 1343.
[17]Paul O'Brien, *Crossfire: the battle of the Four Courts, 1916*, (Dublin, 2012), pp 42-3.

Tom Smart did so and reached safe quarters after bluffing his way through a number of military checkpoints. His Bureau of Military History witness statement is concerned only with the events of Easter 1916.[18] He returned to the volunteers when they were reorganised after the rising and served as a member of the 1st battalion which was the position he held when he joined the DFB.

Michael Joseph Rogers was born in Capel Street, Dublin but was reared by his grandmother in Donard, Co. Wicklow. He married at the age of nineteen and returned to live in Dublin. His bride was Chrissie Quigley of Harold's Cross whose family were originally from Donard. Michael got a job as a tram driver with the Dublin United Tram Company. Following five weeks unpaid training he was employed as a spare driver, expected to turn up at the depot each morning at 7 a.m and wait until noon to see if he was needed on that day. He was only paid for days he worked. In 1918 he applied for, and secured, a position as a fireman with Dublin Fire Brigade.[19]

Austin McDonald was from Mayo and had been a member of the Louisburgh company of the West Mayo Battalion of the Irish volunteers.[20] While there he was engaged in field training, collecting arms and manufacturing munitions. Captured by the police, he injured a number of RIC members in the course of his arrest and served a prison sentence in connection with this from 9 December 1918 to the end of June 1919. Moving to Dublin on his release he worked initially as a shop assistant. He joined the 4th Battalion of the Dublin brigade and was a member of 'A' company. During the period when he was a member of Dublin Fire Brigade he listed among his IRA activities 'regular armed patrols', 'engaged in ambush on enemy troops on Rathmines Road', 'activities in connection with Belfast boycott', 'protective patrols under arms', and 'raids for British Government material'. This was the life of an

---

[18]A follow up letter from Comdt. R .J. Feely asks him to carry it forward from the reorganisation of his unit to the truce but no such witness statement was made. Feely to Smart, 26 May 1949 (Smart family papers).

[19]*Irish Press,* 7-12 November 1960.

[20]Pension statement under 1934 Military Service Pensions Act.

active IRA man in Dublin at the period. Within the DFB he made friends with Joe Connolly. His sister Bessie was later to marry Matt Connolly, Joe's brother and an active member of the Citizen Army.[21] The fact that he had served a prison sentence for Republican activities prior to joining the DFB and that that did not disbar him from joining was indicative of a pro Republican attitude within the Dublin Corporation and indeed the DFB itself.

The influence of these men within the DFB can perhaps be seen in a photograph from the *Chicago Sunday Tribune* of 15 August 1920 which shows the response of the DFB to a fire involving military stores. Part of the IRA campaign involved incendiary attacks on British military property. While these attacks are sometimes seen as insignificant in the overall campaign in Ireland, it should be remembered that the British

'Dublin firemen grin as Military Stores Burn'. The fireman marked 'x' (3rd from right) is Thomas Smart. Beside him (2nd from right) is Joe Connolly.
(Photo: Smart family papers).

[21]Email from Mike Connolly, 30 October 2008.

military and police were in competition for resources with campaigns being waged at the same time in other parts of the British Empire. The British army was heavily committed in both India and Iraq and required large numbers of transport vehicles, and armoured cars to escort them, in both countries. Every vehicle and piece of equipment which could be destroyed in Ireland was hard to replace and helped the rural IRA flying columns to counter the mobility of British forces and tie them down in static garrisons with reduced patrolling capability. All military equipment which could be destroyed added to the ongoing logistical problems of the British Army's Irish Command.

Events in Dublin brought the DFB into daily contact with the war being waged on the streets. Members of the Squad, ASU and intelligence officers of the various city battalions carried on a clandestine war with the state forces who by now included the British army, military intelligence agents, secret service agents, the DMP's G men, the Auxiliary Division of the RIC (ADRIC) and members of counter intelligence groups like the 'Igoe gang'. This group was centred on Head Constable Eugene Igoe of the RIC who led a group of undercover policemen from the country districts sent to Dublin to identify IRA men from the provinces who were operating in, or passing through, Dublin.[22] For many IRA men of the period the Auxiliary Cadets or 'Auxies' of ADRIC were the primary threat. Recruited from ex-military commissioned officers and heavily armed, operating in companies of one hundred men, the Auxiliaries were formidable opponents and were in many ways the first unit of what we now call 'special forces' to operate in Ireland. 'F', 'I' and 'J' companies were stationed in Dublin. A fourth company, 'Q' company, was later established from ex-naval officers and tasked with searching ships in Dublin port for arms and contraband.[23]

Another group who were considered a major threat to the IRA's leadership and structure in Dublin was a British secret service unit known as the 'Cairo gang'. IRA intelligence gathered information on their

[22]Dwyer, *The squad*, pp 201-5.
[23]William Sheehan, *Fighting for Dublin: The British battle for Dublin 1919-1921* (Cork, 2007), p.

Firemen, soldier and police at the aftermath of a street ambush.
(Photo: Courtesy of James Langton).

addresses and it was decided to kill as many as possible of their agents on Sunday 21 November 1921. Michael Rogers was on duty in Tara Street that morning and recalled the tension among DFB members who were aware of the planned operation.[24] As the operation swung into effect IRA units made up of the ASU and local battalions with a stiffening of Squad members moved in on their targets. Twelve British officers, mainly intelligence officers, were shot that morning as were two Auxiliary Cadets. Cadets Garniss and Morris were intercepted by one of the assassination squads as they made their way to Beggars Bush barracks to raise the alarm.[25] The bodies of those killed were removed to King George V hospital by DFB ambulance.

[24] *Irish Press,* 8 November 1960.
[25] Sheehan, *Fighting for Dublin,* p. 160.

Later that afternoon Crown forces, including a large contingent of Auxiliaries, entered Croke Park, where a challenge football game was taking place between Tipperary and Dublin. They opened fire on the crowd and inflicted heavy casualties including fourteen dead. Again the DFB ambulances were dispatched and among the crews who attended were Michael Rogers and Ned Doyle on the reserve ambulance and Joe Connolly and Michael Buckley on the motor ambulance.

The day which became known as 'Bloody Sunday' had still not run its savage course. In the guardroom of Dublin Castle three Republican prisoners were killed by their captors. Dick McKee and Peadar Clancy were senior IRA officers who had helped plan the shootings which had taken place that morning. Conor Clune was a low level member of the Republican movement from county Clare who was in Dublin on business in connection with the Republican loan which was used to fund the separatist movement. He had been arrested earlier that day in a raid. All three were killed by Auxiliaries in what was described as 'an attempt to escape'.[26]

The DFB were once again called on to face the results of the ongoing revolution on 11 December 1920. A call was received from Cork city asking for help with major fires which had been started in the city. Cork city and county was an area of heavy fighting and on 28 November the British forces in Ireland had one of their largest reverses of the Irish revolution. The West Cork flying column under Comdt. General Tom Barry ambushed an Auxiliary mobile patrol at Kilmichael near Macroom. Eighteen Auxiliaries were killed in the ambush, with no survivors.[27] It was a war of reprisal and counter reprisal. After another ambush on the Auxiliaries at Dillon's Cross in Cork City at 4 p.m on Sunday 11 December, the Crown forces launched raids on the homes of Volunteers and, operating in what appeared to be a well planned action, started major fires in the centre of Cork.[28]

[26]Tim Pat Coogan, *Michael Collins* (London, 1990), p. 161.
[27]Tom Barry, *Guerilla days in Ireland* (Dublin, 1955), pp 30-40.
[28]Gerry White and Brendan O'Shea, *The burning of Cork* (Cork, 2006), pp 190-4.

Tara Street Firemen L-R Back: Austin McDonald, J. Mc Keown, J. Keane, M. Buckley, Joe Connolly, Front: J. Murphy, Ned Doyle, J. Kane, L. Barton, N. Seaver, child N. McLoughlin (Photo: DFB Museum)

The Cork City Fire Brigade was overwhelmed and a call for assistance was sent to Dublin's Lord Mayor. With his permission Captain Myers called his men together and called for volunteers to go to Cork's aid. Firemen Bernard Matthews, James Barry, Christopher McDonagh, James Keane, Nicholas Seaver, Joe Connolly and Michael Rogers accompanied Captain Myers to Cork by special train which also carried their engine and equipment.[29] The DFB crew did not return to Dublin until Wednesday 15 December. The centre of Cork was in ruins to rival Dublin in 1916.

[29] *Irish Press,* 9 November 1960.

Oil on canvas painting dated 1903 of a Dublin Fire Brigade turn out to a fire.
(Courtesy of the Mulvaney family).

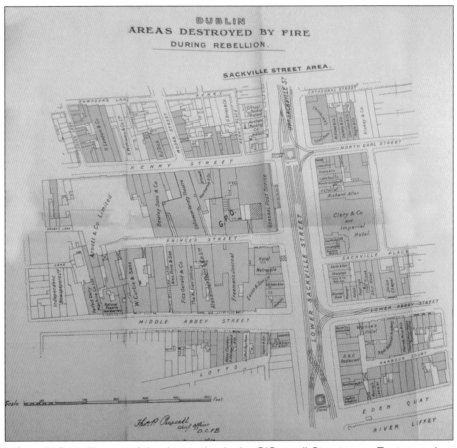

Captain Purcell's map of the destruction in the O'Connell Street area, Easter week 1916. *(Courtesy of the Purcell family).*

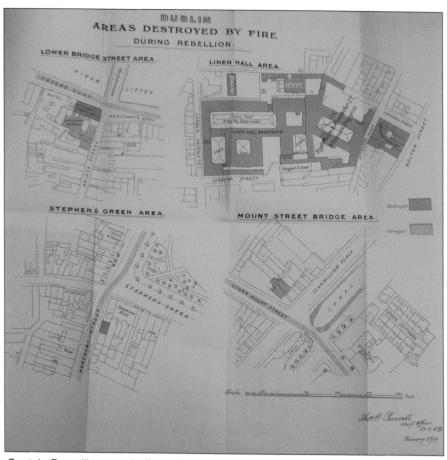

Captain Purcell's map of affected areas 1916. The fire on Usher's Quay was started by Tom Smart and Peadar Clancy to drive a unit of Dublin Fusiliers out of that strongpoint, from which they had been firing on the Four Courts/ Church Street area. Clanwilliam House was destroyed as part of the battle at Mount Street Bridge. *(Courtesy of the Purcell family).*

1914	LOCATION	OWNER	TRADE	LOSS	Remarks
Feb 4	Sackville St	Chambers	Vacant	£ 600	
March 14	Grangegorman	Blake	Spirit Merch	600	
April 12	Essex St	Durdon	Tenement	500	
June 22	Mayor St	Potter	Waggon Works	4,290	
Oct 27	Anne St	Anderson &	Cabinet Works	5,660	
Dec 18	Brunswick St	Harding	Rubber Tyres	670	
	A number of fires Incendiary and others attended in County				
1915	Townsend St	Shanks	Garage	£ 788	
March 24	Mountjoy Sq	Cole	Residence	550	
May 4	Westland Row	D.S.E.R	Office	780	
16	Bride Street	Boyd	Stores	1,220	
17	Abbey St	Armstrong	manufactory Stationers	33,400 ✳	
June 24	Strand St	Baxendale	Ironmonger	626	
	Six fires attended in County				
Nov 12	Kingstown	Gas Works	Flood	Pumped out	

1916

May 24th Rebellion in Ireland

many fires extinguished from Monday evening to noon on Thursday 27th when Shelling of Sackville Street by Military Commenced, fires started on East Side burned unchecked until 5 a.m Friday. From 9 a.m on Friday 28th until 8 P.m on Saturday 29th Post Office side burned. Brigade then got to Work all through Saturday night and stopped all further extension of fires.

Captain Purcell's notes on the Rebellion from his private papers.
(Courtesy of the Purcell family).

Area burned over

	Square yards
East Side of Sackville Street	24.000
West do do	44.900
Linenhall District	29.140
Ushers Quay	1.020
Harcourt Street	135
Clanwilliam Place	225
Total	99.420

Total number of establishments destroyed 186

" Valuation for rating purposes £25.003

(G.P.O. R. Irish Academy Presbyterian church Barracks)
not rated

Approximate estimated value of buildings as they
stood (not present inflated cost to restore 40% higher)

£950.000

do do Contents about   850.000
                       1.800.000
add 40% to cover /   720000
increase in values /
Total Loss due to Fires only   £2.520.000

Chief Officer Purcell's estimates of the damage, Easter week 1916.
(Courtesy of the Purcell family).

Postcard showing the 'new fire station in Brunswick Street' 1907. The station was soon known as Tara Street as the postbox was on that frontage.
(Author's collection).

Dublin firemen grin as military stores burn. The fireman marked marked with an X (third from right) is Tom Smart. Beside him (2nd from right) is Joe Connolly.

(Courtesy Colm Smart).

Dublin Fire Brigademen's Union badge
1892. (DFB Museum).

Medal awarded to members who took
part in the Merryweather Fire Escape
Exhibition in Dublin in 1895.
(DFB Museum).

Royal Humane Society medal awarded
to Fireman Edward Doyle for the 'War
Cypress' incident 1918.
(Courtesy of the Doyle family).

King's Police Medal awarded to Fireman
Doyle for his heroism at the 'War
Cypress' incident in 1918. This was the
highest bravery award made to a Dublin
fireman up to that date.
(Courtesy of the Doyle family).

In Dublin the war continued and the report of an IRA officer after a street ambush in Great Brunswick Street on 14 April 1921 gives an indication of the level of cooperation from some members of the DFB. After giving an account of the ambush, in which two Auxiliaries and three IRA volunteers were killed, he stated that he had received a report of both side's casualties and the names of men captured:

> *This information I received from the driver of the Fire Brigade ambulance who states that 2 men were taken up dead at the corner of Sandwith Street and from a conversation overheard in King Georges hospital.*[30]

In early 1921 Oscar Traynor, officer commanding the IRA's Dublin brigade, was called to a meeting of the IRA's Army Council. Also present were Michael Collins, Cathal Brugha, Richard Mulcahy and the other members of the IRA's general headquarters staff. The meeting was addressed by Eamonn de Valera who stressed the importance of a major action in Dublin to bring public opinion abroad to bear on Ireland.[31] The action decided on by the Dublin brigade, after examining the available targets, was the destruction of the Custom House. The building was entered and examined by Traynor himself, armed only with a large envelope with 'O.H.M.S' on the front.[32] The other officer involved in the process was Comdt. Tom Ennis of the 2nd Battalion. The Customs House stood in his battalion area and the main responsibility for the action would fall on his men. Plans of the building were secured by the engineers of the 5th Battalion and a decision was reached to burn the building on 25 May 1921. The destruction of the building was to be carried out by Ennis's men with assistance from members of the ASU and the Squad. The building was to be destroyed by fire. Each man moving into the building at the appointed hour would carry a can of paraffin which would arrive by truck at the rear entrance. Paraffin was the preferred accelerant to start the fire as petrol fumes mixed with air would

---

[30]W.H. Kautt, *Ambushes and armour The Irish rebellion 1919-1921* (Dublin, 2010), p. 207.
[31]Oscar Traynor, BMH witness statement W.S. 340, pp 67-8.
[32]'On His Majesty's Service' This was stamped on all official envelopes.

form an explosive mix. It appears that the IRA unit planning the operation discussed it with at least some members within the DFB. In Austin McDonald's papers he mentions that he 'assisted with preparations for the total destruction of the Customs House'. The Custom House and the immediate area would be secured by IRA units and, when the building was saturated, the fires were to be lit and all units would withdraw.

Due to a mix up with the signals to withdraw, most of the attackers were still in the building when a lorry of Auxiliaries with an armoured car arrived in Beresford Place and were engaged by the IRA units holding the perimeter. A major gun battle ensued as British reinforcements arrived and surrounded the now burning building. IRA casualties came to six killed and nearly eighty captured.[33]

While the operation was very costly to the IRA's Dublin brigade, it did demonstrate that they could operate at will and were capable of striking at any target they chose including major government centres in the heart of Dublin.

A major element of the planning which went into the destruction of the Custom House was the question of neutralising the Dublin Fire Brigade to prevent it from attacking the fire effectively in its early stages. According to Traynor's account the fire stations were to be held up by local units and the engines disabled.[34] In the case of DFB headquarters in Tara Street the job was given to 'K' company of the 3rd Battalion. While no accounts exist for the take over of Buckingham Street or Dorset Street fire stations, and the take over of Thomas Street is mentioned only in passing in the chief officers annual report, there are a number of accounts of what happened in Tara Street;

[33]Oscar Traynor, BMH witness statement W.S. 340, pp 71-5; Sheehan, *Fighting for Dublin*, pp. 53-4.

[34]Oscar Traynor, BMH witness statement W.S. 340, p. 71.

On Wednesday, May 25th, at 1.05 p.m. a section of the IRA entered the Central Fire Station. The officer in command said he had orders to 'hold up' the station for one hour. Simultaneously the three sub-stations were raided and the same order given in connection with Thomas Street Station. A party of IRA took the motor engine to Crumlin, and kept it there for about an hour. At 1.45 a telephone message was received notifying occurrence of fire in [the] Custom House. Brigade was still prevented from turning out. At about 1.50 the IRA officer commandeered one of our motor ambulances and drove off with his men, ordering us not to leave the station for ten minutes. The ambulance was returned later by one of our drivers who was compelled to drive. A few minutes before 2 p.m., a force of Auxiliaries arrived and directed the attendance of Brigade at outbreak in Custom House.[35]

That is the official account of Captain John Myers to the waterworks committee. Michael Rogers remembered;

A clean cut chap of about 25 sauntered into Tara Street Fire Station. He struck up a conversation with Station Officer Christopher Kelly. I wasn't close enough to catch his words, but I moved a little nearer as, one by one, seven more men slipped in the gate and the last man locked it behind him. Then the clean-cut chap announced in a firm tone 'Nobody leaves here for 15 minutes after a fire call comes through.' As he spoke his right hand moved to his coat pocket in which unmistakably bulged a Parabellum.[36]

The IRA held the station and monitored calls. The officer in charge of 'K' company recalled in an article in a reunion booklet in 1947 how they were aided in their work by IRA intelligence officers in the DFB.[37]

---

[35] *Dublin Fire Brigade Annual Report for 1921*, pp. 21-2.

[36] *Irish Press*, 10 November 1960.

[37] K. Coy. 3rd Batallion 1st Dublin Brigade Old IRA, *Souvenir Programme of Service Certificate*, Saturday 22nd March 1947, DFB Museum, Accession No. 032/08.

The New York Times reported that an official report from Dublin Castle had told how the fire stations, including the Rathmines brigade, were held up by armed men and how, at the Thomas Street station, 'six men, attired in firemen's uniforms, boarded a big engine and drove it off to an imaginary fire.'[38]

On arrival at the fire in the Custom House the Brigade could see that they faced a difficult, if not impossible, task. The actions taken by a number of firemen at this point probably sealed the fate of the building. Michael Rogers tells how, on entering the building to search it and establish the seat of the fire, he and others had the building at their mercy and spread the fire into parts of it which had not previously been on fire. During this operation the firemen found four IRA men still in the building. Rogers was requested to return to Tara Street and bring back spare firemen's shirts and caps. Dressed in these, the IRA men were smuggled out of the building and driven away in fire brigade vehicles from the cordon of military and Auxiliaries who now surrounded the area.[39] R.M Fox in his history of the Irish Citizen Army speaks of how;

> *Members of the Citizen Army in the Dublin Fire Brigade helped to destroy the traces of those who had fired the building. Capt. M. Kelly went in dressed as a fireman and recovered upwards of twenty weapons left by the Volunteers when, surprised by enemy forces, they had to dash out. These weapons were returned to the Dublin Brigade.[40]*

Harry Colley, the adjutant of the 2nd Battalion's 'F' Company, visited the scene at the Custom House on the evening of the fire to try and ascertain the extent of damage and the success of the operation. He found 'a fireman with his hose trained on the fire, but his jet of water falling on the footpath outside. He was being remonstrated with by an Auxiliary officer but he persistently refused to go closer'.[41]

---

[38] *New York Times,* 27 May 1921.
[39] *Irish Press,* 11 November 1960. Geraghty and Whitehead. *Dublin Fire Brigade*, p.169.
[40] Fox, *Irish Citizen Army,* pp 209-10.
[41] Harry Colley, BMH witness statement W.S. 1689, p. 83.

DFB aerial ladder arriving at Customs House 25 May 1921. *(Author's collection).*

In the immediate aftermath of the Custom House attack, and in an attempt to cover the losses incurred by the IRA in the action, the Dublin brigade stepped up incendiary attacks on British government and military targets. The annual report for 1921 lists a number of fires involving attacks on British military stores and transport. The largest of these fires occurred on 3 June 1921 when the National Shell Factory on Parkgate Street was burned with a loss of 'a large number of motor cars, lorries etc. undergoing repair. Fire extended to Ordnance Depot also carpenter's shop and tyre store'.[42]

Dublin firemen played a minor but significant part in the last act of the drama. A small group of DFB men were used to provide security and crowd control at the Mansion House on 8 July when representatives of the British forces and the IRA met to agree terms for a truce to come into effect at noon on 11 July 1921. Negotiations for a treaty were about to begin.

[42] *DFB Annual Report* 1921, p. 21.

Firemen removing wounded in Beresford Place after the Custom House attack.
Auxiliaries with drawn revolvers on right.
(Courtesy of the National Library of Ireland).

Fire at National Shell Factory, June 1921. British army crew with manual fire engine.
(Courtesy of the National Library of Ireland).

CHAPTER 5

Civil War, Dublin 1922

THE euphoria which followed the truce on 11 July 1921 brought new hope to the country. As the details of the treaty between Great Britain and Ireland were published, that hope dissipated for many. A split in the Republican movement formed between those who saw the treaty as a stepping stone to a possible future republic and those who viewed the placement of the new Free State within the British Empire as a sell out of the principles for which they and their comrades had fought.

For a brief period life for the DFB returned to normal. A number of members with long service retired and new members were recruited to replace them. Among the new recruits were John Darmon and Nicholas Bohan. Both were IRA members and both were members of the 3rd Battalions 'K' Company, the unit which had taken over Tara Street for the burning of the Custom House. They were both mechanics and could drive and were classed as 'motor mechanic / driver / firemen'.[1] Captain Myers wanted the Brigade to be fully motorised as soon as possible and preference was given to men with experience of working with motor engines.

John (Jack) Darmon had only been released from Ballykinlar internment camp in December 1921. He had been a member of the Volunteers since 1918 and was a very active member of 'K' company where he had been the transport officer. His employment as a delivery man with Burney Brothers of Pearse Street gave him the use of a pony and trap which was at the disposal of the unit. On one occasion he was responsible for removing an arms dump from Millers of Sandwith Place to a new dump in Kimmage. He had been notified at 6.15 p.m of a raid due to take place at 7 p.m and immediately removed the company's arms to a place of

---

[1] *Dublin Corporation annual report* 1923, vol.i, p.75.

safety. He had also taken part in raids for arms and other Volunteer activities and was on duty on 21 November 1920 as part of the Bloody Sunday pre-emptive strike on British intelligence officers in the city. He was rounded up in the days after Bloody Sunday and was interned in Ballykinlar until the general release of Republican internees in December 1921.[2]

The political situation deteriorated throughout the country as British forces evacuated posts which were taken over by local pro-or anti-Treaty republicans. The Treaty was accepted by the Dáil on 7 January 1922 by a vote of sixty-four votes to fifty-seven. A Provisional Government was set up to administer the new Irish Free State. The IRA itself split, with many units following the lead of their local commanders in terms of which side to support. In the main fighting areas in the south the IRA units declared against the treaty as did most of the Dublin brigade. Within the Dublin brigade itself there was a split with the squad and active service units (now amalgamated as the Dublin Guard) following Michael Collins and the Free State, as did much of Tom Ennis` 2nd Battalion. The remainder of the IRA structure in the city was overwhelmingly anti-Treaty.

On 26 March, IRA leaders met in an army convention and voted to repudiate the Treaty. They also set up an Army Executive headed by Liam Mellowes and Rory O`Connor. On 14 April the anti-Treaty IRA took over the Four Courts and several other buildings around Dublin. This was seen as a direct affront to the Provisional Government. In other areas of the country fighting had been narrowly averted between anti-Treaty IRA units and Provisional Government troops of the new National Army. These localised confrontations had led to uneasy truces in Limerick and other areas.

On 18 June 1922, the people of the new twenty-six county state went to the polls to deliver their verdict on the pro and anti Treaty sides. The pro-Treaty side, with support from other parties won a narrow majority of the vote.

---

[2]Darmon, Application for pension under the Military Service Pensions Act 1934.

Events started to accelerate. On 22 June Field Marshall Henry Wilson was assassinated in London by a two man IRA team. Wilson was a security advisor to the new Northern Ireland parliament and was held by many republicans to be a hard liner and tolerant of attacks on the Catholic community in Northern Ireland by loyalist groups and elements of the police. The attack was assumed by the British authorities to be the work of the anti-Treaty or 'Four Courts' IRA and they prepared plans to attack the Four Courts if the Provisional Government did not act against them.[3] At this time British troops were concentrated in the Dublin area as the process of handing over military facilities and evacuating troops continued throughout the twenty-six counties. On 27 June the Four Courts IRA arrested a National Army officer, General J.J. 'Ginger' O'Connell, in retaliation for the arrest of one of their officers by Free State forces. An ultimatum was delivered to the Four Courts garrison to surrender to the Free State army or face attack. In the face of a refusal to surrender by the Four Courts garrison, the National Army opened fire on

The Four Courts burning, 28 June 1922. *Illustrated London News.*
(Author's collection).

[3]Robert Kee, *Ourselves alone* (London,1987), pp 164-5.

the building and the anti-Treaty forces that held it. Eighteen-pounder artillery pieces were supplied to the Free State government by the British Army to facilitate the assault on Gandon's eighteenth century architectural masterpiece. An offer of gun crews to fire the weapons was refused as the Free State army contained many ex-servicemen who had experience of using artillery in the Great War. The attack commenced at seven minutes past four on the morning of 28 June 1922.[4] For the first time since the Easter Rising, artillery was being used on Dublin streets.

The political situation in the city had added to the workload of the DFB in the early months of 1922. On 30 March armed men set fire to the premises of the *Freemans Journal* at no. 6 Townsend Street.[5] The premises were badly damaged and the reels of paper and machinery destroyed.

The events at the Four Courts on 28 June and the week after were to provide the DFB with its busiest week since Easter 1916. When the attack on the courts complex commenced, IRA units in other parts of the city abandoned a number of isolated outposts and concentrated in larger garrisons. As the IRA units moved out they set fire to the premises to deny them to National Army troops. The first to be set ablaze was the Orange Order's Dublin headquarters at Fowler Hall in Rutland Square. Later that day a premises at 32 Dolphin's Barn which 'had been occupied by armed men' was put to the torch.[6]

Joe Connolly's activities in the early days of the Dublin fighting are worth studying. On 29 June units of the Dublin IRA occupied buildings in Upper O'Connell Street. They were led by Oscar Traynor and Cathal Brugha. Among the units which occupied this block of buildings, which included the Gresham and Hammam hotels, was the Irish Citizen Army.[7] An internal IRA document from shortly after the Dublin fighting describes the ICA in Dublin as comprising two hundred men divided into

---

[4]Dorothy Macardle, *The Irish Republic* (London, 1968), p. 678.
[5]*Dublin Fire Brigade annual report, 1922*, p. 21.
[6]*DFB annual report*, 1922, p. 30.
[7]Liz Gillis, *The fall of Dublin* (Cork, 2011) p. 57.

north and south city sections.[8] They were relatively well armed with their weaponry listed as '20 PPs, 4 P.Bs and 80 other weapons, mostly .45 calibre'.[9] Among the ICA contingent in the Hammam Hotel was fireman Joe Connolly. In his statement under the Military Service Pensions Act[10] Connolly describes himself being 'on active service in the Hammam Hotel O'Connell Street and city of Dublin'.[11] In Connolly's statement he describes 'attacks on the Hammam Hotel defended by myself and others'. Also on duty in the area and fighting on the Republican side was fireman Austin McDonald. McDonald had absented himself from the DFB and reported to 'G' Company of the 4th battalion 'in defence of the Four Courts garrison'.[12] He saw active service in the Tramway Offices and in the Hammam, Gresham and Granville hotels.

The 'Block', as the group of building in Upper O'Connell Street was called by those defending it, came under heavy attack from National Army forces. According to family historian Mike Connolly, who has access to his uncle Matt's contemporary journal, Joe was called by Oscar Traynor and ordered to return to his post in the fire brigade 'where he could be of better service doing ambulance work, bringing wounded from the Four Courts and carrying important messages'.[13] He certainly did return to the brigade as he was on ambulance duty the following day when he took an ambulance in to the Four Courts and removed a wounded Republican senior officer.

At the Four Courts a temporary ceasefire had been called to allow the wounded to be tended. One of the wounded Republicans was Paddy O'Brien, officer commanding the Four Courts garrison. He was high on

---

[8]Brian Hanley, *The IRA; a documentary history 1916-2005* (Dublin, 2010), p. 47.

[9]'PP' in this context stands for Peter the Painter', IRA slang for a Mauser C 96 automatic pistol. 'PB's were Luger parabellum pistols. Both weapons were highly prized by the IRA.

[10]Application for pension, Military Service Pension Act, 1934, signed by 'Jos. Connolly', dated 3.5.38. (Connolly family papers.)

[11]While the name of the hotel was the 'Hammam', it is often refered to as the 'Hamman'.

[12]Austin McDonald, Application for pension, Military Service Pensions Act, 1934.

[13]Mike Connolly, South Africa, email, 30/10/2009.

the list of men wanted by the Free State authorities. O'Brien was removed from the Four Courts by a DFB ambulance driven by Joe Connolly.[14] After treatment for a head wound at Jervis Street Hospital, Connolly arranged to get him away from the hospital and safely home. Firing appears to have continued even during the temporary ceasefire as Fireman Nicholas Bohan was reported in the *Irish Independent* as having had his clothing struck by a bullet which passed through them.[15] The available evidence would suggest that Connolly (Citizen Army) was accompanied by Nicholas Bohan (IRA) on an ambulance at the Four Courts which removed at least one senior Republican. In the BMH witness statement of Laurence Nugent, an officer of 'K' company of the IRA's 3rd Battalion, he states that 'Jack Darmon, K Coy., an ambulance driver at the Tara Street Fire Brigade Station, removed an important individual from the Four Courts as a casualty. This person was not wounded'.[16] Jack Darmon's own statement in support of his application for a pension under the 1934 Military Service Pensions Act mentions removing a man from the Four Courts and also mentions removing Jack Rooney from Aughrim Street to Pembroke Road. John Rooney was a member of the IRA's 1st battalion. By removing him from Aughrim Street to the south side of the city he was being taken outside the Free State army's cordon around central Dublin. Darmon also mentions the assistance of firemen James McKeown and James Markey in removing these men. The evidence is that the ambulance crews which responded to the Four Courts were made up largely of committed Republicans and acted as couriers for messages in and out of the Four Courts at the very least and may have assisted the escape of some members of the garrison. Jack Dorman, in his application for a pension under the 1934 Military Service Pensions Act, clearly describes his Civil War activities:

> *'owing to [the] nature of my employment I rendered all possible service to my comrades.'*

---

[14]Annie O'Brien, Lily Curran, joint witness statement to BMH WS 805 p. 37.
[15]*Irish Independent,* 30 June, 1922.
[16]Laurence Nugent, BMH witness statement, WS 907, p. 279.

The cinema ambulance during the battle for Dublin 1922.
Illustrated London News (Author's collection).

By 30 June, the position of the Four Courts garrison was untenable. A massive explosion had shaken the building which had been under artillery fire for over two days. The Irish Public Records Office and its historic files and documents were destroyed in the explosion which had forced the evacuation of that side of the complex. Ernie O'Malley, officer commanding in the absence of Paddy O'Brien, received word that the Republican forces outside were unable to come to the relief of the Four Courts garrison. This message appears to have been delivered at about the time that the DFB ambulance was removing Paddy O'Brien. A decision to surrender was inevitable and O'Malley surrendered to General O'Daly of the Free State Army.

At 11.15 a.m the DFB received a call from police telephone 851 to the effect that firing had ceased at the Four Courts and they turned out all available men and appliances.[17] Captain Myers and his men laid hose to try and fight the fires but it was an impossible task. Exploding munitions

---

[17] *DFB annual report 1922, p. 30.*

made the work hazardous. Captain Myers approached Rory O'Connor, the Republican leader, then a prisoner under guard, and was warned that there were approximately seven tons of explosive material within the building. Myers ordered his men to withdraw but before they could do so three firemen were injured when munitions exploded. The Brigade's efforts were confined to preventing the spread of fire into adjoining buildings and to dealing with a series of fires in the surrounding area caused by burning material blown from the Public Records Office in the earlier explosion there.

Papers and manuscripts being picked up in O'Connell Street after the Four Courts explosion. *Illustrated London News (Author's collection).*

There were a number of serious fires in the city over the following days related to the heavy fighting which was still going on. In one case at Guiney's shop in Talbot Street, the fire had originated in a street barricade outside the building. Among a number of fires in the city on 2 July was an outbreak at Augustine Street at which thirty-six barrels of turpentine belonging to the Nugget Polish Company had to be removed from the path of the flames. On 3 July, the Brigade turned out to the Lucania Cycle and Engineering Works in Pleasants Street.

Having dealt with the fire at the Lucania Works, the Brigade were sent later that day to Upper O`Connell Street to a fire at the Y.M.C.A building. This building, which was strongly barricaded, was in an area of intense fighting as Free State forces moved in on the 'Block' in Upper O`Connell Street. The firemen laid hose to the fire and had extended the aerial ladder from Buckingham Street station when they were forced to withdraw due to the intensity of rifle and machine gun fire. A number of bullets struck the ladder on which firemen were working and the vehicle had to be abandoned until early the following morning, when a crew from Buckingham Street was able to retrieve it during a lull in the fighting.[18] The Brigade returned to the Y.M.C.A. building later on 4 July.

Captain John Myers at the YMCA fire, O'Connell Street.
(Courtesy of the National Library of Ireland)

[18]*DFB annual report* 1922, p. 23.

Republican forces in O'Connell Street were now concentrated in one small area at the upper end of the north eastern corner, mainly comprising the Hammam, Gresham, and Granville Hotels.

On 5 July, in the face of overwhelming numbers of Free State troops and artillery, the Republican garrison abandoned the 'Block' leaving just a small rearguard under Cathal Brugha. Among the Republican garrison in the Block who escaped from the area was Eamonn De Valera. In a number of reputable works it has been suggested that he was smuggled away by ambulance but there is no specific mention of him from the DFB members involved in smuggling away other Republicans.[19] The whole area was now in flames with the DFB attempting to control what Captain Myers described as a 'conflagration involving the northern end of Sackville street.'[20] Among the tactics used by the Free State troops was to throw cans of petrol into the lower parts of the building to accelerate the fire.[21] Brugha ordered the rearguard to evacuate the building and surrender but he stayed behind. The lane at the side of the burning hotel was crowded with firemen attempting to stop the spread of the flames. It was also filled with Free State troops. When the Republican rearguard left the building it was realised that Brugha was still inside. What happened next is described in Laurence Nugent's witness statement:

> *'Two of the firemen smashed some doors with hammers. One of these men was Lieut.Bohan, a member of 'K' coy. He states that when the door was opened Cathal Brugha came out with a revolver in each hand and commenced firing on a party of Free State soldiers who were in the lane. The fire was returned and Cathal Brugha fell mortally wounded. The firemen lifted him up and he said 'Firemen, I'm finished.' . . . the brigade was called elsewhere and saw no more of this incident.*[22]

---

[19]Tim Pat Coogan, *Michael Collins*, (London, 1990) p. 387, James Durney, *The civil war in Kildare*, (Cork, 2011) p. 75.

[20]*DFB annual report*, 1822, p. 33.

[21]Laurence Nugent, BMH witness statement, WS 907, p. 279.

[22]*DFB annual report 1922*, p. 34.

Cathal Brugha, one of the legendary figures of the 1916 Rising, died of his wounds two days later. Again one of the IRA members within the Brigade can be placed at the scene of a pivotal incident.

When the main fighting finished the Brigade was able to concentrate its resources. The conflagration in Upper O'Connell Street was out of control and continued to spread. It was helped in this by the Republican tactic of knocking holes in the walls of adjoining buildings in the block in order to move freely without attracting attention or small arms fire. The fire spread through several buildings and reached Findlaters. It was stopped at this point. Myers and his firemen were very much aware that among the stock of Findlaters were thousands of gallons of whiskey which would be a major fuel source for the fire if it got that far. The same consideration on a larger scale concerned Gilbeys spirit merchants which was in the path of the blaze. What Myers described as 'the most critical period of the whole of the fire-fighting was spent to prevent the involvement of Messrs. Gilbeys. Many thousands of gallons of various liquers were stored in their extensive vaults. Fortunately we were successful, leaving the the building safe and comparatively untouched by fire'.[23] The Pro Cathedral also received the brigade's special attention and a line of hose was played on the walls and doors nearest to the fire. In Myers words: 'This ediface was saved'.[24] The last major fire related to the fighting was in the Dublin Corporation workshops in Stanley Street which had been occupied by Republicans. A hint of the old inter service rivalry can be seen in Myers report: 'Blaze rapidly spread. Laid two lines of hose and saved one wing. Rathmines Fire Brigade attended, but, fortunately, their services were not required'.[25] In total eighty buildings were destroyed or partially destroyed in the battle for Dublin.

[23] *DFB annual report 1922*, p. 34.
[24] *DFB annual report 1922*, p. 34

After the end of organised Republican resistance in Dublin the focus of the Civil War moved elsewhere. The Free State forces consolidated their positions throughout the country and attacked the Republican stronghold in the 'Munster Republic' both on land and by assaults from the sea on a number of key positions. Within Dublin the fighting reverted

Fire engine and crew waiting for the ceasefire, 5 July 1922.
(Author's collection).

to the hit and run tactics of the war against the British. Again it became an intelligence war and a small unit war of ambush and assassination. The new Free State government was determined to impose its will and, after the death in an ambush in county Cork of Michael Collins, the new regime imposed severe penalties on opponents caught in arms against the state. The death penalty was to be imposed on any person found in possession of arms. The first to die under this new sanction were four

[25]Geraghty and Whitehead, *The Dublin Fire Brigade,* p.147.

Dublin IRA members, James Fisher, Peter Cassidy, John Gaffney and Richard Twohig who were executed by firing squad in Kilmainham on 17 November 1922.[26] In December, in response to the assassination of a member of the Dáil, the Free State government decided to execute four prisoners in their custody since the surrender of the Four Courts. Rory O'Connor, Liam Mellows, Joseph McKelvey and Richard Barrett faced the firing squad on 8 December 1922. The Civil War would drag on until May 1923, an increasingly bitter struggle which scarred the country for generations to come. Austin McDonald states in his pension application that he ceased to be active around this time 'because of aversion to any further fratricidal strife'.

After the exhausting work of early July, the DFB reverted to the normal duties of firefighting and ambulance work. War-related fires continued on a sporadic basis however and on 11 August the Brigade had a section held

Tom Smart driving RI 1090, the Tara Street Leyland, in Michael Collins' funeral procession *(Courtesy Colm Smart)*

[26]Martin O'Dwyer, *Seventy seven of mine said Ireland* (Cork 2006), pp 18-24.

up by armed men as they made their way to a fire in Amiens Street Post Office. The crew from Buckingham Street was ordered to drive to the North Circular Road. The fire in Amiens Street was dealt with by two other sections.[27] A series of fires in railway signal cabins in September and October appear to have been an attempt to interfere with railway communications as part of a national campaign by anti-Treaty forces against the railway system. Attacks on tax offices were orchestrated on 1 November with fires at 21 Merrion Street Upper at 1.43 p.m and 16 and 17 Sackville Street Lower at 1.45 p.m. On 5 November the temporary General Post Office at the Rotunda Rink was raided and burned in a large fire which gutted the premises. The Rotunda Rink had been in use since 1916 to replace the GPO in O'Connell Street. Arson attacks continued

DFB crew 1922. Back row: 1st right, Nicholas Bohan,
2nd right, Patrick Bruton, 3rd right, Thomas Smart. *(Photo: Smart family papers).*

[27] *DFB annual report 1922*, p. 23.

through November and December with further fires in railway signal cabins (19 November), tax offices (22 November), the homes of T.D. Sean McGarry and Postmaster General J.J. Walsh (10 December) solicitors (two attacks on 12 December) and finally on 31 December the premises of W.L Cole T.D, fruit merchant, was burned by incendiaries.[28]

In the attack on the home of Sean McGarry at Philipsburg Avenue three women, including Mrs. McGarry, were held at gunpoint while armed men spread petrol. This was ignited in spite of the women's protests that there were children in the house. Emmet McGarry, aged 7, died of burns later in hospital having been rescued from the house along with his sister. Another child had escaped during the raid.

The work of the Brigade during the fighting in Dublin at the start of the Civil War was officially recognised by the Dublin Corporation in 1923. Each man on duty for the full period was awarded a chevron with the attendant one shilling per week pay rise. In addition, in Dublin Corporation Annual Report no. 86 of 1923 each man was rewarded as follows; Captain Myers £30, Second Officer John Power £20, each station officer £10, and each qualifying fireman £5. Each man was also to be given one week's additional annual leave. Two firemen were excluded from this payment which was not to extend to anyone 'absent with or without leave'. Neither Joe Connolly nor Austin McDonald are on the list.

The new state was established, peace had returned to the country, the Brigade could return to normal duty. The revolutionary years were over.

---

[28] *DFB annual report 1922,* p. 27-8.

CHAPTER 6

Conclusion

THE development of the Dublin Fire Brigade as a municipal fire service in the last decade of the nineteenth and the first years of the twentieth century is a tribute to the leadership and vision of the chief officer, Thomas Purcell. Parallel to this technical advancement however is the human story of the men and their families who made up the workforce of the brigade. Their trials and tribulations, their attempts to organise and advance their claims to a decent standard of living, are also part of the history of Dublin.

Growing from that well of organised labour one can also trace a separatist element. From faint beginnings in Easter Week 1916 with the actions of trade unionist and Citizen Army man Joseph Connolly, we find evidence of other activists who became members of the brigade and played a part in the Irish Revolution.

It is, of course, difficult to trace the activities of men engaged in gathering information and offering clandestine help to a secret army in an undercover war. This study has relied on written and verifiable sources and a lot of anecdotal evidence has had to be discarded because it cannot be referenced against any other source. The primary sources used, especially the witness statements of the Bureau of Military History and pension statements under the Military Service Pensions Act, were examined with a critical eye. Gathered in a period beginning in 1948 in the case of the BMH statements, the historian must always bear in mind that these are the memories of men and women looking back at those earlier days through the prism of a bitter civil war. In the case of this study it was found that the activities of the firemen and the fire brigade were incidental memories to many of those who made the statements and certainly do not appear coloured by later events.

The previously unknown photo from the *Chicago Tribune,* which turned up among the papers of Thomas Smart, and for which I am indebted to his son, retired District Officer Colm Smart, was an exciting find. This photo, while obviously staged for propaganda effect (and noticeable for the absence of an officer) was still strong evidence of the strength of feeling within the brigade at that period. If nothing else it could have been construed at the time as photographic evidence of dereliction of duty by all concerned and would have resulted in major disciplinary action by the brigade or Waterworks Committee. To have willingly posed for that photograph was in itself an act of solidarity with the revolution.

It is not the aim of this book to present the members of the Dublin Fire Brigade as essential elements of the revolutionary movement without whose efforts it could not have succeeded. Rather it is to show how, in conjunction with many others, in the civil service, post office, prison service etc., and very many ordinary men and women in every walk of life, they contributed to the essential undermining of British rule in Ireland in those years. The firemen, by the nature of their occupation, sometimes had access to information denied to others and often used that access for the advancement of the revolution. In other cases it can be shown that they played a more active role and their activities during the Custom House attack are those of active participants rather than bystanders.

The aim of this study was to throw light on an overlooked area of the revolutionary years, the role of ordinary people who may never have taken part in an ambush or held a gun but whose actions undermined the rule of the British administration. They withdrew their consent from one government and gave it instead to a new and untried entity, the Irish Republic.

The men involved in this study all went on to serve long and honourable careers in the Dublin Fire Brigade. Joe Connolly served as Chief Officer of the Brigade before he retired in 1937. Jack Darmon lost his life in a tragic line of duty accident in Tara Street in 1938. On the night of 15/16 April 1941, Michael Rogers was one of the officers who took fire engines to Belfast at the request of the Northern Ireland government to assist in fighting the massive fires caused by a German air raid on that city. The raid happened at Easter, the twenty-fifth anniversary of the 1916 Rising.

BIBLIOGRAPHY

(A) Primary sources

Manuscript sources

> Bruton / Houghton family papers
> Connolly family papers
> Purcell family papers
> Smart family papers

Department of Defence, Veterans Affairs section, Galway

> Applications for pension under Military Service Pensions Act, 1934.

> Connolly, Joseph
> Darmon, John
> McDonald, Austin
> Smart, Tomas

Military Archives, Cathal Brugha barracks, Dublin.

> Bureau of Military History witness statements:

> Colley, Harry, W.S 1689.
> Good, Joseph, W.S 388.
> Hackett, Rose, W.S 546.
> Nugent, Laurence, W.S 907.
> O'Brien, Annie and Curran, Lily, (joint statement) W.S 805.
> Oman, William, W.S 421.
> O'Shea, James, W.S 733.
> Smart, Thomas W.S 1343.
> Traynor, Oscar, W.S 340.

Printed sources

(a) Official reports

Dublin Fire Brigade Annual Reports 1870-1923 (available at NLI)
Dublin Corporation Annual Reports 1862-1923 (available at Dublin City Archives)
Dublin Corporation Minute Books 1890-1923

(b) Newspapers and periodicals

Chicago Sunday Tribune
Cork Examiner
Freemans Journal
Irish Independent
Irish Press

Irish Times
Irish Worker
New York Times

Brigade Call
Fire
Firecall
Fire and Water
The Fireman

(c) Oral sources

Connolly, Mike. Interview by phone 1/10/10
Geraghty, Tom. Interviews 4/6/10 and 24/ 9/10
Rogers Vincent. Interview   6/9/10
Smart, Colm.   Interview 7/9/10

(B) Secondary sources;

Abbott, Richard, *Police Casualties in Ireland 1919-1922* (Cork, 2000).

Ambrose, Joe, *Dan Breen and the IRA* (Cork, 2006).

Bailey, Victor, *Forged in fire: the history of the fire brigades union* (London, 1992).

Barry, Tom, *Guerrilla days in Ireland* (Dublin, 1955).

Baumer,Edward, *The early days of the Sun fire office* (London,1910).

Blackstone, G.V., *A history of the British fire service* (London, 1957).

Breen, Dan, *My fight for Irish freedom* (Tralee,1964).

Broadshurst, William, & Walsh, Henry, *The flaming truth: a history of Belfast fire brigade* (Belfast, 2001).

Carroll, Lydia, *In the fever king's preserves: Sir Charles Cameron and the Dublin slums* (Dublin, 2011).

City of Dublin Vocational Educational Committee, *The old township of Pembroke 1863-1930,* (Dublin, 1993).

Coogan, Tim Pat, *Michael Collins* (London, 1990).

Cox, Ronald, *Oh Captain Shaw* (London, 1989)

Dublin Corporation, *Opening of the new central fire station* (Dublin,1907).

   -----   *Historical souvenir: the Dublin fire brigade 1862-1937* (Dublin, 1937).

Durney, James, *The civil war in Kildare* (Cork, 2011).

Dwyer, T. Ryle, *The squad* (Cork, 2005).

Fox, R.M., *History of the Irish citizen army* (Dublin, 1944).

Foy, Michael T., *Michael Collins intelligence war* (Stroud, 2006).

Geraghty, Tom, & Whitehead, Trevor, *Dublin fire Brigade: a history of the brigade, the fires & the emergencies* (Dublin, 2004).

Gillis, Liz, *The fall of Dublin* (Cork, 2011).

Golway, Terry, *So others might live: a history of New York's bravest: the FDNY from 1700 to the present* (New York, 2002).

Griffiths, Kenneth, & O'Grady, Timothy, *Curious Journey: an oral history of Ireland's unfinished revolution* (Dublin, 1998).

Hanley, Brian, *The IRA: a documentary history 1916-2005* (Dublin, 2010).

Herlihy, Jim, *The Dublin metropolitan police* (Dublin, 2001).

---- *The Royal Irish constabulary: a short history and genealogical guide* (Dublin, 1997).

Holloway, Sally, *London's noble fire brigades 1833-1904* (London, 1973).

---- *Courage High: a history of firefighting in London* (London, 1992).

Hooper, Glenn, *The tourist's gaze* (Cork,2001).

Jackson, W. Eric, *London's fire brigades* (London, 1966).

Kautt, W.H., *Ambushes and armour: the Irish rebellion 1919-1921* (Dublin, 2010).

Kee, Robert, *Ourselves alone* (London, 1987).

Kenneally, Ian, *The paper wall: newspapers and propaganda in Ireland 1919-1921* (Cork,2008).

Limpus, Lowell M., *History of the New York fire department* (New York, 1940).

Maclysaght, Edward, *Forth the banners go* (Dublin, 1969).

McArdle, Dorothy, *The Irish republic* (London, 1968).

McNally, Michael, *Easter rising 1916: birth of the Irish republic* (Oxford, 2007).

Nelligan, David, *The spy in the castle* (London,1968).

Novick, Ben, *Conceiving propaganda: Irish nationalist propaganda during the first world war* (Dublin, 2001).

O'Brien, Paul, *Blood on the streets: 1916 & the battle for mount street bridge* (Cork, 2008).

----- *Uncommon valour: 1916 & the battle for the south Dublin union* (Cork, 2010).

----- *Crossfire: the battle of the Four Courts,1916* (Dublin, 2012).

O'Dwyer, Martin, *Seventy-seven of mine said Ireland* (Cork, 2006).

O'Maitiu, Seamas, *Dublin's suburban towns 1834-1930* (Dublin, 2003).

O'Malley, Ernie, *On another man's wound* (Dublin, 2002).

Poland, Pat, *Fire call* (London, 1977).

---- *For whom the bells tolled: a history of Cork fire services 1622-1900* (Dublin, 2010).

Prunty, Jacinta, *Dublin slums 1800-1924: a study in urban geography* (Dublin, 1998).

Radford, Fredrick H., *Fetch the engine: the official history of the fire brigades union* (London, 1951).

Robbins, Frank, *Under the starry plough: recollections of the Irish citizen army* (Dublin, 1977).

Sheehan, William, *Fighting for Dublin: the British battle for Dublin 1919-1921* (Cork, 2007).

Supple, Barry, *The royal exchange assurance: a history of British insurance 1720-1970* (London, 1970).

Various authors, *Dublins fighting story* (Cork, 2009).

   ---   *The Sinn Fein rebellion handbook* (Dublin, 1998).

Wallington, Neil, *In case of fire: the illustrated history and modern role of the London fire brigade* (Huddersfield, 2005).

White, Gerry, & O`Shea, Brendan, *The burning of Cork* (Cork, 2006).

Whitehead, Trevor, *Dublin firefighters* (Dublin, 1970).

Williams, Bertram, *Fire marks and insurance fire brigades* (London, 1927).

Wright, Brian, *The British firemark 1680-1879* (Cambridge, 1982).

   ---   *Insurance fire brigades 1680-1929* (Stroud, 2008).

APPENDIX A

IRA and ICA members who served in the DFB post 1923

In the years after the Civil War a number of men with Irish Republican Army and Irish Citizen Army service joined the DFB. Some did not join until the early 1930s when a change of government signalled a change in official policy towards employment of men who had fought on the anti - Treaty side in local government and state jobs. Others joined the DFB in the period immediately after the Civil War and under the administration of Chief Officer John Myers. Myers was followed as chief officer by John Power, the first fireman to rise from the ranks to lead the Brigade and he in turn was succeeded by Joseph Connolly, himself a Citizen Army veteran. After Connolly's retirement in 1938 the chief officer's job was given to an army officer, Major J.J. Comerford. Comerford had also fought in the Civil War. He had joined the Free State army as a lieutenant in the Railway Protection Corps in 1922.

The following list is the result of many years of research. In some cases full records of the service of the individual are available but in others, only bare details survive. The author would welcome any further details on the pre 1923 Republican service of any of the men listed or indeed any other firemen from the period who may have been overlooked in my research.

William Carroll, born 20 April 1901. Joined Irish Citizen Army September, 1917, served to May 1918. Joined 'G' Company 1st Battalion, Dublin Brigade IRA. Transferred by Peader Clancy to battalion cycle scouts and was attached to battalion intelligence from September 1920 to Truce. Took anti-Treaty side and was acting O.C 'J' Company, 1st Battalion during Civil War. Took part in attacks on Free State Army. Joined Dublin Fire Brigade 18 May 1924.

George Connolly, (Brother of Joseph Connolly). Irish Citizen Army, City Hall garrison 1916. Involved in capture of guard room Dublin Castle, Easter Monday. Active with Citizen Army throughout War of Independence. Transferred to 5th Battalion (Engineers) Dublin Brigade IRA during Civil War. Captured by Free State Army and interned. Joined Dublin Fire Brigade 1923.

Denis Fitzpatrick, born 17 April 1900. Four Court garrison 1916. Member 'B' Company, 1st Battalion Dublin Brigade IRA. Took part in reorganisation of company after the Rising. Transferred as Captain, 'E' Company, 3rd Battalion, Scottish Brigade IRA, March 1919 to February 1920, in charge of collecting arms and explosives in Stirlingshire. April 1920 returned to 'B' Company Dublin Brigade. Attached 'B' Company and Active Service Unit (ASU), Dublin Brigade. After Truce commissioned in Free State Army. Resigned from Free State Army and returned to Irish Republican Army prior to attack on Four Courts 1922. Took part in actions at Fowlers Hall, Barry's Hotel and Dorset Street. Shot and seriously wounded. Served as intelligence officer and was involved in plan to tunnel into Mountjoy to free Republican prisoners. Captured and interned at Hare Park Camp, Curragh. Joined Dublin Fire Brigade 3 March 1932.

Patrick Kelly, born 23 February 1891. Member Transport Worker Union 1913, dismissed during Lockout for refusing to handle goods delivered under police protection. Joined 'G' Company 1st Battalion Dublin Brigade early 1916. Fought in Four Courts garrison 1916. An accomplished marksman, he was engaged in counter sniping during the fighting in the Four Courts / Church Street area which saw some of the heaviest fighting of the Rising. After the surrender he was interned in Frongoch. On release he returned to 'G' Company and was active in arms raids and street ambushes during the War of Independence. Took anti-Treaty side and was involved in the fighting in the Parnell Square and Capel Street areas. Captured by Free State Army during the battle of Dublin, 1922. Joined Dublin Fire Brigade 2 August 1926.

Robert Malone, Member 'D' Company 3rd Battalion Dublin Brigade. Bolands Mills Garrison 1916. Deported to Frongoch after surrender. Joined Pembroke Fire Brigade and was transferred to Dublin Fire Brigade on the amalgamation of the townships and Dublin Corporation in 1930. Stationed at Tara Street fire station, he lost his life on 5 October 1936 while fighting a fire at a tenement in Pearse Street. Firemen Nugent and McArdle were killed at the same incident. Robert Malone's application for a pension under the Military Service Pension Act 1934 is due to be released into the public domain as part of the release of documents held under the act prior to the centenary of the 1916 Rising. It was not available at time of writing.

Daniel O'Dowd, born 5 April 1903. As a teenager witnessed the surrender of the Marrowbone Lane / South Dublin Union garrison in 1916. Joined the Fianna initially and then the Volunteers and served briefly with the 4th Battalion. Transferred to the 3rd Battalion and was active with them during the War of Independence. In Four Courts garrison prior to the attack on the Courts at the start of the Civil War. Transferred to Masonic Hall, Molesworth Street and after the evacuation of that post he was active with a small unit which sniped at Free State troops in Beggar's Bush barracks. His unit also sought targets of opportunity among the evacuating British military in order to provoke a reaction from them. Captured in a raid by Free State troops, he was interrogated for three days by Free State intelligence officers / C.I.D in Oriel House. Imprisoned in Mountjoy and Hare Park camp, Curragh. Dan O'Dowd was a noted uilleann piper and became a legend in traditional music circles. Joined Dublin Fire Brigade 14 November 1928.

James Scully, born Dublin 15 May 1899. He joined the Liverpool Batallion of the IRA in 1919 and was involved in a number of actions there including arson attacks on warehouses and cutting telegraph wires to disrupt communications. He also took part in attacks on the homes of Black and Tans and Auxiliaries whose addresses had been located as a result of raids on the mail in Ireland. Came back to Dublin in May 1922 and joined the Four Courts garrison. He was captured and interned after the fall of the Courts. Joined Dublin Fire Brigade 20 June 1932.

APPENDIX B

Firefighting arrangements in County Dublin 1880-1923.

W.N. Hancock, writing in the Journal of the Statistical and Social Inquiry Society of Ireland in 1882 reviewed 'arrangements for putting out fires in Dublin City and the townships of Drumcondra, Clontarf, Kilmainham, Pembroke, Rathmines, Blackrock and Kingstown'. These were the areas within the county of Dublin in which any organised arrangements for firefighting were in place. In Hancock's review he found various arrangements in place. He speaks highly of the city brigade and compliments the late Captain Ingram for his work. Then he turns his gaze on the townships.

In terms of fire escape ladders, Kingstown had one and Pembroke had one on order. There were two hose reels in Pembroke and one each in Blackrock and Kingstown. Dalkey and Clontarf had hose and nozzles but no hose reel car to carry them. Rathmines had a modern steam fire engine and one old hand pumped engine. Of the other townships only Kingstown owned a fire engine. Pembroke had an eight man fire brigade and there was a brigade in Rathmines.

His general findings were that only one township had an escape ladder, one had both a brigade and a fire engine, one had a brigade without a fire engine and one had a fire engine without a brigade. Three had hose reel cars with hose and nozzles, two had hose and nozzles without hose reel cars to carry them and two had a high pressure water system but neither hose nor nozzles to use it.

This then was the situation within the area controlled by the Corporation and the townships. What of the then largely rural area which today makes up the South Dublin County Council area? In Ireland generally at this time there were few fire brigades outside the major cities and a few major towns. In some areas fire brigades, of varying efficiency, were maintained by local industries such as mills, breweries and distilleries. Others were maintained by local institutions or large estates. These would usually be made available to fight fires in the locality if only for the practice it offered in using the equipment. Localities with a military barracks might also benefit from the service of the barracks fire picket and, finally, all recruits to the Royal Irish Constabulary underwent a course in firefighting as part of their recruit training at the RIC depot in the Phoenix Park. When posted to the various RIC barracks in the country they would have at least some knowledge of firefighting although usually no access to firefighting equipment beyond buckets and one man hand pumps.

Large areas had no fire cover of any sort. In the case of the South Dublin County Council area at this time no organised fire brigades can be identified operating within the area. It has to be assumed that some high risk businesses had at least some basic firefighting equipment. The norm at this time was to request a catalogue from Shand Mason, Merryweather, or one of the other fire equipment manufacturers or agents and buy whatever level of equipment and uniform which was considered necessary or which might be insisted on by an insurance company as part of the terms of their policy. On occasions the DFB sold off surplus equipment and in 1910 the Spa Hotel, Lucan bought a fire escape ladder from the brigade. This was one of the Clayton wheeled escapes which were obsolete within the city as they would not fit under the overhead tram wires which had been a feature of central Dublin since 1898.

In the period covered by this book there were a number of fires recorded within the present S.D.C.C area. To access help from the DFB the owner of the premises had to contact the Chief Officer of the DFB or the Lord Mayor of Dublin. Premises outside the Corporation area were not entitled to the attendance of the DFB as a right. The procedure was to send a message by telegram requesting the presence of the DFB. After consultation and depending on an agreement to pay the appropriate scale of charges, a section of the brigade would be dispatched. Due to a refusal to travel too far outside the city boundaries, in order not to expose the city to danger, the actual number of turnouts was quite small.

In 1892 the DFB attended one fire in the modern SDCC area, at the Clondalkin paper mills. In 1893 they attended a fire at a farm at Baldonnell. It was 1899 before the DFB again attended a fire in the area and again it was a paper mill, the Boldbrook paper mill in Tallaght. That was a busy year as they also attended fires at a stables in Saggart and a fire at Finnstown House. 1900 found the DFB at a fire in a three storey tenement in Palmerstown. In 1902 the brigade returned to Clondalkin paper mill on 5 October but refused to travel to Rathcoole on 20 November.

A fire at Maynooth college, Kildare, on Christmas Eve 1904 was attended by sections of the DFB transported there by special train. No payment was recorded for this attendance. In 1907 they attended a fire at the Dominican Priory in Tallaght and in 1908 a fire at the Carmelite Monastery in Clondalkin. In 1910 the DFB attended a fire at Lucan House, the home of Captain Vesey.

These quiet years ended in 1913 with an increase in fires in agricultural produce in the county area. Many of these were in connection with the Lockout and involved retaliation for the use of scab labour rather than unionised agricultural labourers.

The following years were again quiet until a fire in the Monastery in Clondalkin on 26 April 1917, followed by a fire in Peamount Sanatorium on 2 August of that year. 1918 was a busy year with fires in Lyons House, Hazelhatch on 10 May, Hermitage Golf Club on 7 June, a wheat store at Gollerstown, Lucan on 6 September and a fire involving seven tons of burning rags at Salmon Leap Mills, Leixlip on 23 November. In 1919 no fires are recorded in what is now the South Dublin County Council's area.

Events in Ireland in 1920 are reflected in the annual fire reports. A decision to keep the brigade within the city seems to have been reached. Fires in Clondalkin on both 4 September and 8 September were not attended. More interestingly the brigade did not respond to the sack of Balbriggan either. The event being recorded in the annual report for that year as: 'September 21 Balbriggan, Outbreak due to armed incendiarists. Did not attend'. A fire in Lucan on 24 November was not attended either.

In December, following an appeal from the Lord Mayor of Cork, a section of the brigade under the chief officer was despatched to that city to fight the fires caused by Crown Forces in retaliation for the Dillons Cross ambush and for the earlier Kilmichael ambush. A special train was laid on to carry the men and equipment. The train took a long time to arrive in Cork as Irish railwaymen were in dispute at this time as the railmen's union were refusing to carry British military personnel, equipment or munitions. The train needed a special dispensation to travel south. The value of the railwaymen's actions and the strain it placed on British military transport and logistics is often overlooked in the story of the fight for freedom. A note on the times by the chief officer in the annual report remarks that :

> *'fortunately there have been no 'curfew' accidents, so far, to members of the brigade'.*

This was a period when many civilians and prisoners in military and police custody were shot 'trying to escape' from curfew patrols and the custody of the Crown forces.

The last major 'out of area' fire fought by the DFB during the period under review came following a phone call from President Cosgrave of the Free State government on 29 August, 1922. The brigade was requested to attend a fire at Maryborough (Portlaoise) prison. The fire had been started as a protest by Republican prisoners held there. The brigade responded and again a special train was laid on to carry the men and equipment.

In 1923 there were two fires in the Clondalkin area where the brigade did not attend citing a lack of available water to fight the fires. The brigade was still busy within the city limits with outbreaks of incendiarism in connection with the Civil War. There were twenty recorded incendiary attacks within the city that year, the same number as in 1920 and '21 and there may have been a reluctance to allow the brigade to be left under strength by allowing sections to operate outside the city limits until the risk of civil disturbance or military action was definitely past.

APPENDIX C

543

MEMORIAL.

To the Chairman and Gentlemen of the Waterworks Committee in charge of the Fire Brigade Department, City Hall, Dublin.

GENTLEMEN,

We, the Firemen of the Dublin Corporation Fire Brigade, beg most respectfully to submit this Memorial, which we trust will meet with your ever generous consideration.

Gentlemen, by perusing the following scale of duty, we trust it may give you a fair idea that we are not making an unjust request, and when it is taken into consideration the confined body of men we are, and the disadvantages we are at in comparison to other prominent Brigades in the United Kingdom, it will be seen that our lives are absolutely at the service of the public, with the exception of five hours' leave, which is granted to two men out of each station in their turn on an average of about once a week.

Now, first, we will give you an outline of station duty—take, for instance, a man is called at 6.30, a.m., and comes on duty at 7 o'clock, a.m.; he remains on duty in the station all day till 6 o'clock, p.m.; and if he is for chimney fires that night he remains until 10 o'clock, p.m., and if a chimney fire occurs during he night he will be called out of his bed until the men who attend the same returns, and, no matter how long they may be away, the man who was called out of his bed will be called the same time as the remainder of the men in the morning; should he be for bunk duty that night, which we do on an average every third night, he commences that duty at 6 o'clock, p.m., and remains on duty till 7 o'clock, a.m, the following morning, after being in the station all day from 7 o'clock, a.m., until 6 o'clock, p.m., as aforesaid. The following will, we say, be part of his duty, providing he be the first man of the bunk—gate duty, 6 p.m. to 8 p.m.; telephone duty, 8 p.m. to 10 p.m.; he may rest from 10 p.m. to 12 p.m.; gate duty, 12 p.m. to 2 a.m.; telephone duty, 2 a.m. to 4 a.m., and he may rest from 4 a.m. to 6 a.m.; and again gate duty, 6 a.m. to 7 a.m. This man, it may be seen, gets but four hours' rest out of twenty-four hours, providing there be no fires, chimney fires, or otherwise.

Now, the second man's duty is—gate duty, from 8 p.m. to 10 p.m.; telephone duty, 10 p.m. to 12 p.m.; he may rest from 12 p.m. to 2 a.m.; gate duty, 2 a.m. to 4 a.m.; telephone duty, from 4 a.m. to 6 p.m. *(sic)*—this man has but two hours' rest out of twenty-four hours.

5

544

The third man's duty is—telephone duty, from 6 p.m. to 8 p.m.; gate duty, 10 p.m. to 12 p.m.; telephone duty, from 12 p.m. to 2 a.m ; he may rest from 2 a.m. to 4 a.m.; again gate duty, 4 a.m. to 6 a.m.; telephone duty, 6 a.m. to 7 a.m.; this man, also, has but two hours' rest out of twenty-four hours.

But, Gentlemen, should it occur that any of those men be for duty in Wapping-street or Cardiff-lane on the morning of the day they are for bunk, if, in the summer months, he is called at 5 o'clock a.m., and in the winter months at 6 o'clock a.m., the consequence is that if he is the second man of the bunk, he will be nineteen hours on his feet before he is at liberty to lie down; but should he be the third man of the bunk, and called at 5 o'clock, a.m., he would not be at liberty to rest until 2 a.m. the following morning, which would mean twenty-one hours without resting.

Now, in lieu of this bunk duty which we do, we may go to bed at 7 o'clock, a.m., after being up all night; if we are married we go home until 12 o'clock, noon, that means we may get 4 hours' rest. Well, Gentlemen, there are some who may get it, but it would be as well for others to remain where they were, as they have to wait until some member of the family gets up before they can go to bed, owing to the size of the apartments, there being no room but for one bed, as some of the rooms are only fifteen feet long by nine feet wide—scarcely fit for one to live in, much less a family, this being station duty.

Now, with reference to escape duty, the following is the scale : We parade in the station at 7.20 p.m., and in the summer months we return at 6.20 a.m. the following morning; in the winter months, from 7.20 p.m. to 7.20 a.m. Now, Gentlemen, should a fire occur during the day, which is often the case, or if we have to get up at 2 p.m. to go home with an escape, or shift escapes, or if there is a general drill, we get up at 11 a.m.; a man very often gets but a few hours' rest, and has again to face the night; and should a man be found in the escape-box by our Chief, it is ten chances to one it is not made a crime of, as he says we must not enter the boxes except it is raining, but if we are tired to sit on the lever of the escape. Well, in the London Brigade, when the men go on escape duty, they are allowed to go to bed in their clothes in the boxes, and when they return the following morning, after the appliances are cleaned, they go to bed proper. Now, surely, if such a great body of men are allowed to do that, we feel certain that the Committee will allow us to use the boxes whenever we feel tired; and if we are found accidentally dosing in the small hours of the morning, as long as we are sober and capable of doing our duty, that it will not be made a crime of.

Well, Gentlemen, we have now given you a true statement of

6

110

545

our duty ; and, as we said before, it is a rule we get five hours'
leave in our turn, which occurs, on an average, about once a
week. Of course, we will not deny that we can get a day's leave
now and then, but it is not a standing order ; therefore we don't
like to ask for it at times, for fear we might be refused. And
we also have to give particulars of where we are going. But,
Gentlemen, we will give you a sketch of the leave granted to
other prominent Brigades. Now take, for instance, the Man-
chester Brigade. Each man in his turn gets twenty-four hours'
leave, which occurs every thirteen days, and seven days' annual
leave in the summer. Now, take the London Fire Brigade. Of
course they cannot be put on a par with any other for their leave
and the manner in which they are housed ; their pay and pensions far exceed any other. But when it is taken into consideration the number of men that are in the London Brigade,
and the population, if they were divided according to the population of this city, it will be seen that there would be over
eighty to the number of inhabitants there instead of our number
of forty-four ; and taking into consideration that a first-class
fireman's pay in London is 37s. 6s. per week. Of course we will
not attempt to put ourselves on a par with the London Brigade ;
but there are stations in London that do not attend as many
fires as we do, and, most assuredly, they don't do the hours of
duty we do, but nevertheless their pay, leave, and prospects of
pensions are the same as a fireman in the heart of the city. But,
Gentlemen, as we have no pensions, we venture to say that the
Committee will be unanimous in granting us the following
concessions :—

1st. That a first-class fireman's pay be 30s. per week, and the
remaining classes in proportion.

2nd. That the scale of leave be henceforth that two men from
each station in their turn be granted leave from
5 o'clock, p.m., to 11 o'clock, p.m., which will occur on
an average about once a week, and seven days' annual
leave during the year ; and that a man be permitted
to change with another if it may not be suitable for
said man to take leave at the time, or if a man requires a day's leave for important business it be
granted to him. Also, that a man may go on leave
in plain clothes whenever his leave comes due.

3rd. That a man does but one month's night duty at a time ;
for when we do night duty we have no leave whatever, and it often occurs that we do two or three
months' night duty running, which is not necessary,
as it could be arranged otherwise.

4th. That there be an improvement made in the married

7

546

    they are totally inadequate for the housing of a family,
quarters, as in some cases, as we have before stated.

5th. That the hours of escape duty be from 8 p.m., to 6 a.m. all the year round.

6th. That when a man is brought before the Committee for an offence, he shall be allowed to give a personal explanation, and call witnesses in his defence, and also for him to be furnished with a copy of the Report that is about to be produced against him.

7th. That the present arrangement of testing the escapes be abolished, viz. :—It has come into practice lately that when an escape is brought from Messrs. Brown, or brought into the yard for drill, there are several men placed on it, one after another, by way of a test.   Now, Gentlemen, as you are aware, all the escapes have been tested in your or the City Engineer's presence by weight only, and not by men ; therefore, if they are to be tested again in future, let it be in the way you witnessed.

8th. That the men of the Fire Brigade be granted a pension after twenty-one years' service, as we are certain that the Committee will agree with us in saying that a man deserves some recompense after devoting the best years of his life and all his energy in the service of the public.

Finally, Gentlemen, we earnestly request you to put a stop, once and for all, to the petty tyranny that we are continually subjected to ; it is time enough to be spoken to when we commit ourselves   We do our duty, as the past can prove ; therefore, we strongly object to be continually hagged at.   And trusting, kind Sirs, this our Memorial will meet with your ever-generous consideration,

      We beg most respectfully to remain,

        Your obedient servants,

    THE MEN OF THE DUBLIN CORPORATION FIRE BRIGADE.

      (Signed),

        [Forty-two signatures follow.]

APPENDIX D

THE FIFTY-FOURTH
ANNUAL REPORT

FROM

THE CHIEF

OF THE

DUBLIN CORPORATION

Fire Brigade Department

For the Year ending 31st December, 1916.

DOLLARD, PRINTINGHOUSE, DUBLIN,
WELLINGTON QUAY.

1917.

2

Waterworks and Fire Brigade Committee,
1916.

Appointed under the Acts 24th & 25th Vic. and 41 Vic.

RIGHT HON. SIR J. M. GALLAGHER, LORD MAYOR,
ex officio.

Councillor LENNON, Chairman.

,,   M. J. MORAN, Deputy-Chairman.

,,   ROONEY.

,,   O'HARA.

.,   BROHOON.

,,   GROOME.

.,   PARTRIDGE.

,,   M. O'CONNOR.

Alderman O'CONNOR.

,,   COTTON, M.P., D.L.

Secretary—CHARLES POWER.

Medical Officer—DR. J. H. M'AULEY.

Veterinary Surgeon—G. L. RICHARDSON, M.R.C.V.S.

3

FIRE DEPARTMENT.

ANNUAL REPORT FOR THE YEAR 1916.

To the Chairman and Members of the Waterworks Committee.

GENTLEMEN,

I have the honour to present the Fifty-fourth Annual Report on the work of the Fire Department for the year ending 31st December, 1916.

The Brigade received 145 calls to normal fires or supposed fires—a decrease of 76 calls and 61 fires as compared with previous year. Of these calls

100 were fires in the City.

  7 were to fires outside the City.

 23 were to chimney fires.

  3 Houses which had fallen.

 12 False alarms, of which all but two from sprinklered systems were maliciously given.

In addition to above there was unfortunately the abnormal fires, several amounting to serious conflagrations, due to looting of shops and military operations consequent on the rebellion during the last week in April.

Of the ordinary fires four with losses over £500 are classed as serious, thirteen medium with losses between

4

£50 and £500, and eighty-three slight. The total estimated value at risk in these fires is estimated at £465,733, and the losses ascertained after settlements by Insurance Companies £41,209.

The rebellion losses are being dealt with by The Property Losses Commissioners, ex gratia payments and awards by way of compensation to sufferers are made by the Government, and not yet completed, no accurate estimate is therefore available. An approximate estimate of the direct losses to buildings and contents due to the fires alone would be about £2,000,000.

With the exception of three children who were locked in during their parents' absence and rescued by civilians who broke the windows before arrival of brigade, there were no lives endangered by fire during the year.

Exclusive of the disturbed period when the Brigade was practically at work continuously, it " turned out " to fires with motors and other appliances 93 times— 42 during the daytime and 51 at night.

Of 17 fires recorded in appendix, 12 occurred at night, 11 being in closed premises, entrance to which had to be forced.

In addition assistance was asked for and rendered outside the City as follows :—

1. June 8th, at 10.56 a.m., Steam Ship " Lord Antrim," in Alexandra Basin.—Fire originated amidships in woodwork on starboard side, caused by oil lamp, extinguished by a line of hose from hydrants, damage slight.

5

2. August 22nd, at 2.31 p.m., Bray.—Received call by 'phone from Town Clerk's Office for assistance, proceeded with motor engine and 8 men, travelling over the intervening distance of 12 miles in 22 minutes, on arrival found roof of large Station Hotel burned off and all top rooms alight, placed engine on esplanade and got to work with two effective lines of hose, taking water from the sea, stopped fire from going downwards except six bedrooms on third floor at eastern end, all lower rooms with contents were saved from fire but damaged by water and hasty removal prior to our arrival. Insurance, £18,500. Loss, £10,600. The fire was due to defective construction of a flue. Returned 8.56 p.m.

3. September 24th, at 9.15 p.m., Raheny, 4 miles. —Did not attend, but gave owner instructions over the 'phone how to deal with a bad flue on fire.

4. October 10th, Sutton, 5 miles, at 7.44 a.m., by Railway Signal system.—Motor engine with officer and 5 men attended and found a thatched barn 70 feet long, containing corn in sacks and agricultural implements, practically destroyed. Insured, £450. Loss, £102.

5. October 12th, Kileek, Swords, 9 miles.—Motor engine with officer and 5 men attended at 4.17 p.m., and worked through the night until 6.25 a.m., taking water from a river through two lines of hose (1,800 feet), a quantity of farm produce was destroyed, and a hay shed with other farm offices damaged. Insurance, £1,550. Loss, £880.

6. November 6th, Glenmaroon, Chapelizod, Hon.

6

A. E. Guinness, owner, at 2.40 p.m., in a laundry building of two stories, 60 x 25, with return used as dwelling, extinguished at 5.30 p.m. by a private line of hose worked by staff, and one line from motor engine pumping flood water, roof burned off. Loss, about £150.

7. December 28th, at Victoria House, Dalkey, residence of R. W. Booth, J.P.—Officer and 7 men attended with motor engine and worked from harbour for short period, drowning out fire until tide ebbed, then assisted township men to complete extinguishing of smouldering fires in roof debris which had fallen into top rooms. Fire originated in Mansard roof, which was burned off, and second floor with contents badly damaged, 4.02 to 10.11 p.m. Loss, about £3,000.

FIRES DUE TO REBELLION.

April 24th, Easter Monday.

3.58 p.m., Phœnix Park.—In one section of magazine, 120 x 45, containing large quantity of ammunition, extinguished by one jet from Motor engine working 8 hours, buildings saved, but most of the ammunition in that section destroyed.

10.06 p.m., 31 Sackville Street :—Extinguished fire in "Cable" boot shop (previously looted), by one jet from hydrant.

11.59 p.m., 18 Sackville Street :—Extinguished fire in basement of "True Form" boot shop (looted) by a jet from hydrant.

April 25th, Tuesday.

11.56 a.m., 32 Sackville Street :—Extinguished fire in rear of Dunne's hat shop (previously looted).

7

4.11 p.m., 5, 6, 7 Upr. Sackville Street :—Extinguished fire in Lawrence's fancy goods warehouse with 6 jets from hydrants, three augmented by motors. The place was being looted and in complete disorder, two persons trapped in an upper room by fire and taken down by fire escape proved to be looters. Withdrew after four hours' work leaving men with hose until 12.29 p.m. next day, half of the premises being then saved.

26th, Wednesday.

12.59 p.m., 47 Henry Street—Extinguished fire in Williams & Co.'s store at rear of shop, by a jet from hydrant, building saved but stock looted ; 5 men breaking away when firemen arrived.

5.14 p.m.—Called again to same building, and saved it.

6.59 p.m., North Wall—Jute fire on Quay side, Shipping Co.'s watchman kept fire under by a line of hose, did not attend.

8.07 p.m., 8 Sackville Street—H. E. Taffe, outfitter, did not attend (within the firing lines), house burned down, but fire did not extend.

8.40 p.m., 1 and 2 Clanwilliam Place—Did not attend as the houses were being shelled by military.

27th, Thursday.

5.07 a.m., Harcourt Street—Extinguished fire in shop of four storied building by two jets from hydrants, stairs and part roof destroyed.

9.30 a.m., Linenhall Barracks—In use as Army Pay Department. The resident caretaker reported by 'phone that 32 clerks were besieged and had previously extinguished two outbreaks of fire by means of the fire hose within the premises. A bomb had just then been exploded in rear of the building, and a big fire had started in the theatre a temporary structure from previous exhibition. Could not attend under the conditions prevailing in that section of the city. The barracks were burned down, and fire, which lasted two days and nights unchecked, extended

8

to and burned the extensive adjoining oil and drug stores
of Hugh Moore and Alexander, Ltd., also Leckie and Co.'s
printing works, and three other business houses in Bolton
Street.

12.32 p.m., Abbey Street Lr.—As this, the G.P. . district, was
then under continuous rifle fire and being shelled by
field guns and mortars we could not approach it, con-
sequently, this was really the commencement of the
conflagration which wrought such havoc on the Sackville Street Area.

In twenty minutes the fire, which originated in a street
barricade of paper stock and bicycles, had extended to
both sides of the thoroughfare, through a printing office
on north side into Sackville Place, and through Wynne's
Hotel on the south into Harbour Court, gradually spread-
ing by Hoyte's Corner to the D. B. C. building and by
Hamilton and Long's stores to Eden Quay. At 7.20
p.m. the "May Oatway" detector in Scott's, 2 Lower
Sackville Street, indicated in our Station that fire had
reached that point. During the night fire extended to
Imperial Hotel and Clery's Warehouse, and caught the
new bakery and restaurant of Sir Joseph Downes in
Earl Place.

28th, Friday.

3.05 a.m., Usher's Quay—Turned out the Thomas Street Section
with Motor Engine to an outbreak in Lower Bridge
Street and Usher's Quay corner, and working with two
jets for 8 hours, stopped the spread of fire in this area.
Four houses on Quay together with a tram car and street
barrier were destroyed, and the roofs of four others in
Bridge Street damaged.

5.50 a.m.—I turned out with Tara Street Section to Eden Quay
and Lower Abbey Street, and working 5 lines of hose
stopped fire at Marlboro' Street end before it reached
City of Dublin offices. Also working from Cathedral
Place through rooms above Hickey's and under cover
of that building the fire was extinguished in Downes's

9

shop, prevented from crossing or extending in Earl Street, thus stopping its further progress for that time. Sniping was going on and we returned to Station at 9.30 a.m.

6.40 a.m.—Buckingham Street Section attended and extinguished a fire in 96 Harcourt Street by one jet from hydrant, returning at 9 a.m.

1.16 p.m., Henry Street—Fire reported in rear of Arnott's, Henry Street. As district was being shelled did not attend. Workshop, stable and garage destroyed.

3 p.m.—In the evening fires again started on south side of North Earl Street, in that part of the block north of Clery's, which was left safe in the morning, and crossing by the street barrier of household furniture, caught Tyler's boot shop on N. W. Corner of Earl Street, extending easterly next day through Rowe's drapery to Sheridan's and Nagle's licensed premises.

6 p.m.—Sackville Street, West Side—The General Post and Telegraph Offices which were being shelled, got alight and burned during the night, also Coliseum Theatre and other property adjoining. "May Oatway" automatic detectors recorded in our station at 8.30 p.m. the spread of fire to Eason's warehouse.

29th, Saturday.

3.40 p.m.—Received message from Commander of Troops in Dublin that active military operations had ceased and that I might now make an effort to stop the fires which were then going in Sackville Street, Abbey Street Middle, and Henry Street. Turned out with whole available force and got to work with 4 lines of hose off 2 Motor Engines on O'Connell Bridge taking water from river and four other lines off hydrants, also 2 aerial ladders. The G.P.O., Hotel Metropole Coliseum Theatre, and other adjoining houses were then burned. Eason's and Thom's on the north side, and five houses on south side in Abbey Street from Elvery's Corner, were burning.

After half an hour's work making excellent progress towards stopping the fire, several shots were fired from

10

the direction of Upper Abbey Street, the bullets hitting
the wall near where some firemen were working, immediately afterwards a number of shots came from the
Aston's Quay direction, hitting one engine, six bullets
going through the steel tubes and sides of the ladder on
top.

Called off the men and sent them back to Stations, having
to abandon our engines and some other appliances, and
allow the fires to go ahead unchecked.

5.30 p.m., Earl Street—Received message that Hickey's warehouse
had caught, four men in charge of Lieutenant Myers
attended, and working one line of hose extinguished the
fire with slight damage.

8 p.m., Henry Street—Received message from Jervis Street Hospital
that showers of sparks were falling on the hospital from
fires extending in that direction, the condition becoming
serious for the patients.   Turned out with the whole
force again, also asked for and obtained the assistance
of men and apparatus from Guinness's Brewery and
Power's Distillery, the fires having meantime extended
along both sides of Abbey Street and Henry Street.
Recovered our Engines and got fully to work stopping
the fires in every direction during the whole of the night
until 8 a.m. on Sunday when Brigade returned to quarters.
For six days afterwards frequent attention was given
in cooling down smouldering fires in the ruins.

Sunday, April 30th.

6.25 p.m., Marrowbone Lane Distillery—Extinguished some hay
which had ignited beneath a vat by one jet from hydrant.

Tuesday, May 2nd.

1.15 p.m., 6 Henry Street—Fire originated in the top floor of a
long extension to the rear and communicated with front
portion of house and jeweller's shop (previously looted),
extinguished by two jets from hydrants augmented by
motor.

11

The total number of establishments
   destroyed was   196

Annual valuation for rating purposes £32,000

   Do. do.   of Government Property   £4,525

Not rated nor included—Royal Irish Academy,
   and Presbyterian Church.

Approximate estimate of direct loss by fire £2,000,000

AREAS DESTROYED (SEE MAPS ANNEXED).

	Square Yards
Sackville Street Area	68,900
Linenhall ,, ...	29,140
Lower Bridge Street ,, ...	1,020
Mount Street ,, ...	225
Stephen's Green ,, ...	135
TOTAL	99,420

LIST OF HOUSES DESTROYED BY FIRE DURING REBELLION.

LOWER SACKVILLE STREET.

1—Hopkins and Hopkins, jewellers.

2—William Scott and Co., tailors.

3—Hamilton, Long and Co., apothecaries.

4—Francis Smyth and Son, umbrella manufacturers.

The Waverley Hotel and Restaurant.

5—Great Western Railway of England, offices.

12

6 and 7—Dublin Bread Company Restaurant, popularly known as the D.B.C.

Frank R. Gallagher, cigar merchant.

8—Grand Hotel and Restaurant.

9—E. R. Moore, jeweller.

10 and 11—Charles L. Reis and Co., fancy goods warehouse. The Irish School of Wireless Telegraphy.

12 and 13—The Hibernian Bank.

14—Robert Buckham, gentlemen's outfitter.

15—City and County Permanent Building Society, offices.

16—F. Sharpley, ladies' and children's outfitters.

17—Hoyte and Sons, druggists.

G. P. Beater, architect and civil engineer.

18—The True-Form Boot Company.

19—J. P. Callaghan, tailor and hosier.

20—George Mitchell (Ltd.), cigar and wine merchants.

21 to 27—The Imperial Hotel.

Clery and Co. (Ltd.), drapers' warehouse.

28—Richard Allen, merchant tailor.

29—Frs. O'Farrell (Ltd.), tobacco importer.

30—The Munster and Leinster Bank (branch).

31—The Cable Boot Company (Ltd.).

32—Dunn and Co., hatters.

33—Lewers and Co., boys' clothiers and outfitters.

34—Noblett's, Ltd., sweet shop.

G.P.O. and Telegraph Department.

35—Kapp and Peterson, Ltd., tobacconists.

35 to 39—Hotel Metropole.

39—Henry Grandy, merchant tailor.

40—Eason and Sons, general newspaper and advertising office and subscription library.

41—David Drimmie and Sons, insurance agents.

42—The Misses Carolan, milliners.

43 and 44—Manfield and Sons, boot and shoe manufacturers.

46 and 47—John W. Elvery and Co., waterproof and gutta percha manufacturers.

13

UPPER SACKVILLE STREET.

1—John Tyler and Sons, boot merchants.
2—Dublin Laundry Co. and Dartry Dye Works.
3—John McDowell, jeweller.
4—E. Nestor, milliner.
5, 6, and 7—William Lawrence, photographer and stationer.
8—Henry Taaffe, gentlemen's outfitter.

SACKVILLE PLACE.

11—Vacant. Printer's plant.
13—Corrigan and Wilson, printers.
14—John Davin, wine rooms.
16—Denis J. Egan, wine and spirit merchant.

HENRY STREET.

6—S. Samuel, jewellers, etc.
16—James O'Dwyer and Co., tailors.
17—Harrison and Co., cooks and confectioners.
Joseph Karmel, tailor.
18, 19, and 20—Bewley, Sons, and Co. (Ltd.), provision and general merchants.
21—Irish Farm Produce Co.
22 and 23—E. Morris, merchant tailor.
F. Nicholson, dentist.
24—The Coliseum Theatre.
25—H. E. Randall, boot and shoe manufacturers.
26 and 28—MacInerney and Co., drapers.
27—McDowell Brothers, jewellers.
29—Adelaide Repetto, fancy warehouse.
30—The World's Fair 6½d. Stores.
34—Dundon and Co., tailors and outfitters.
35—A. Clarke and Co., millinery and general fancy warehouse.
36—Madame Drago, hairdresser.
37—E. Marks and Co. (Ltd.), Penny Bazaar.
38—R. and J. Wilson and Co., confectioners and fancy bakers.

14

39 McCarthy and Co., costume and mantle warehouse.
39A—Leonard and Co., chemists.
40—Bailey Brothers, tailors.
40A—Mrs. Charlotte Gahagan, ladies' outfitter.
41A—Joseph Calvert, provision merchant.
41—Patrick M'Givney, cutler and optician.
42—John Murphy, spirit merchant.
43—R. and J. Dick, boot and shoe manufacturers.
44—Caroline E. Fegan and Co., underclothing factory.
49—Menzies and Co., milliners.
50—Hampton, Leedom and Co., hardware merchants.
51—Hayes, Conyngham, and Robinson, chemists.
52—Miss White, milliner.
53—Maples and Co., merchant tailors.

EARL STREET.

1A—James Tallon, newsagent.
1—T. Carson, tobacconist.
2—A. Sullivan, confectioner.
3—J. J. Lalor, Catholic art repository.
4—Philip Meagher, vintner.
5—James Winstanley, boot warehouse.
6—Nouveau et Cie., costumiers.
7—Sir Joseph Downes, confectioner, baker.
25—J. Nagle and Co., wine and spirit merchants.
26—Mrs. E. Sheridan, wine and spirit merchant.
27—Delany and Co., tobacco and cigar merchants.
27A—J. Alexander, merchant tailor.
28—M. Rowe and Co., general drapers.
29, 30, and 31—John Tyler and Sons (Ltd.), boot manufacturers.

MOORE STREET.

1 and 2—J. Humphrys, wine and spirit merchant.
3—O. Savino, fried fish shop.
4—Miss B. Morris, dairy.

15

5—M. J. Dunne, pork butcher.
6—R. Dillon, fruiterer.
59—Francis Fee, wine and spirit merchant.
60—Miss M'Nally, greengrocer.
61—C. O'Donnell, victualler.
62—Miss Ward, victualler.

COLE'S LANE.

1—F. Tierney, hairdresser.
2 and 3—C. Farren, boot warehouse.
4—C. Walsh, furniture dealer.
5—Tenements.
6 to 8—H. Leedom and Co., stores.

LOWER ABBEY STREET.

1—Young and Co., Ltd., wine and spirit merchants.
2—J. J. Kelly and Co., cycle agents.
3—J. J. Keating, cycle and motor dealers.
4—*Irish Times*, Ltd., reserve printing offices.
5—Ship Hotel and Tavern.
6—The Abbey Toilet Saloon, Ltd.
7—John Hyland and Co., wholesale wine merchants.
8—C. G. Henry, wholesale tobacconist.
Presbyterian Church—Rev. John C. Johnston, M.A., minister.
28—Patrick Foley, wine and spirit merchant—damaged.
29—Denis Nolan, private hotel.
30—Francis Marnane, furrier.
31—William Collins, oil importer and hardware merchant.
32—Humber, Ltd., cycle and motor manufacturers, wholesale depot.
32—The *Leader* Newspaper.
32 and 33—Keating's Motor Works.
32 and 33—The Irish Commercial Travellers' Association.
33 and 34—Percy, Mecredy and Co., Ltd., publishers; Irish Homestead Publishing Co.; James M'Cullagh, Son, and Co., wholesale wine merchants; the Royal Hibernian Academy.

16

35, 36, and 37—Wynn's Hotel.

37—Smyth and Co., Ltd., hosiery manufacturers.

38—J. Ferguson and Co., hairdressers.

39—Peter Callaghan, gentlemen's outfitter.

MIDDLE ABBEY STREET.

62—Patrick Gordon, wine agent, offices.

63—J. Booth, offices.

64—W. J. Clarke, manufacturers' agent.

65—Kevin J. Kenny, advertising agency. " Irish Manufacturers' Directory."

66—W. J. Haddock, ladies' and gentlemen's tailor.

67—Collins and Co., tailors.

68—George Young, builders and general ironmongers.

69 and 70—Sharman Crawford, wine merchant, office building.

71—Dermot Dignam, advertising agent.

73—James Allen and Son, auctioneers and valuers.

74 and 75—Gaynor and Son, cork merchants.

76—Y.M.C.A. Supper Room for Soldiers and Sailors.

78—John J. Egan, wine and spirit merchaat, The Oval.

79 and 80—Eason and Son, Ltd., wholesale newsagents.

81 and 82—Do.

83—*Evening Telegraph* Office.

84—*Weekly Freeman* and *Sport* Office.

85—Sullivan Brothers, educational publishers.

86—Sealy, Bryers, and Walker, printers and publishers.

87 to 90—Alexander Thom and Co., Ltd., Government printers and publishers.

91, 92, and 93—Fitzgerald and Co., wholesale tea, wine, and spirit merchants.

94—The Wall Paper Manufacturing Co.

96—Maunsel and Co., publishers.

96—Francis Tucker and Co., Ltd., church candle and altar requisites manufacturers.

97—W. Dawson and Sons, Ltd., wholesale agents.

17

98 and 99—W. Curtis and Sons, brass and bell founders, plumbers, electrical and sanitary engineers.

100—J. Whitby and Co., cork merchants.

101—John Kane, art metal worker.

102 to 104—National Reserve Headquarters.

105—Perfect Dairy Machine Co.

PRINCE'S STREET.

3—Prince's Stores, licensed.

4 to 8—*Freeman's Journal* (Ltd.).

13—Stores—Printers.

14—Vacant.

15—Pirie and Sons, stores—Paper.

16—Lalouette's Horse Repository.

21 and 22—Arnott's garage and works.

26—Bewley, Sons, and Co., Ltd., garage.

27—Tenements.

28—Hoyte and Sons, Ltd., stores.

EDEN QUAY.

1 and 2—Barry, O'Moore, and Co., accountants and auditors.

3—Gerald Mooney, wine and spirit merchant.

4—The London and North-Western Railway Co., General Inquiry Office.

5—G. R. Mesias, military and merchant tailor.

6—The Midland Railway of England, receiving, booking, and inquiry office.

6—Wells and Holohan, railway and shipping agents.

7—J. Hubbert Clark, painter and decorator.

8—The Globe Parcel Express.

9—Henry Smith, Ltd., ironmonger.

10—Joseph M'Greevy, wine and spirit merchant.

11—The Douglas Hotel and Restaurant.

12—Mr. John Dalby.

13—The Mission to Seamen Institute.

14—E. Moore, publican.

18

MARLBOROUGH STREET.

112—J. Farrell, wine and spirit merchant.
113—Marlborough Hotel.

LOWER BRIDGE STREET.

18—Tenements.
19 and 21—Doherty's Hotel.
20—Brazen Head Hotel.

USHER'S QUAY.

1—H. Kavanagh, wine and spirit merchant.
2, 3, and 4—Dublin Clothing Co., factory.

BOLTON STREET.

57—George Freyne, hardware merchant.
58—D. Dolan, chemist.
59—W. Leckie and Co., printers and bookbinders.
60—Tenements.

YARNHALL STREET.

1—Hugh Moore and Alexander, Ltd., wholesale druggists.
Linenhall Barracks.
4, 5, 6, and 7—W. Leckie and Co.'s workshops—Printers.

HARCOURT STREET.

96—Norman Reeves, tailor.
97A—Mrs. Elizabeth Bryan, fruiterer.

CLANWILLIAM PLACE.

1 and 2—Private houses.

19

NORMAL CITY FIRES.

OCCURRED IN	WERE CAUSED BY
1 Bakery	2 Airing Linen
1 Brush Manufacturer's	2 Burning Rubbish
3 Cabinet Makers'	4 Children with Lights
1 Chemical Works	23 Defective Construction
2 Forage Stores	3 Electrical Defects
3 Fried Fish Shops	1 Explosion of Spirit Vapour
3 Hotels	
2 Maltsters'	1 Ignition of Escaping Gas
5 Offices	
2 Pawnbrokers' Sale Shops	4 Lamps Upset
	5 Light in Contact
1 Painting Contractor's	1 Light Thrown Down
14 Residences	4 Overheating
1 Soap Manufacturer's	2 Plumber's Blow Lamp
1 Steamship	4 Sparks
7 Stores	3 Spontaneous Ignition
12 Shops, Various Trades	3 Tar and Fat Boiling
1 Timber Drying Kiln	1 Tramp's
1 Textile Works	26 Unknown
3 Tailor's Shops	
27 Tenements	
2 Saw Mills	

STAFF.

The strength of the Staff remains unaltered.

The two members who volunteered on the outbreak of the war are still serving abroad with the Colours, their dependents being allowed half-pay by your Committee. Sgt. Bruton, Irish Guards, who was wounded, is again on active service.

During the year the health of staff was very good, only two men were ill, being absent for 192 days, one of the men is being superannuated ; accidents to 5 men while working at fires entailed an absence of 81 days. Your Chief Officer also was severely injured

20

owing to his horse being out of control when proceeding to a fire at 2.15 a.m., 16th November.

AMBULANCE SERVICE.

This service has been efficiently worked during the year. First aid was rendered by the Firemen on many occasions. Assistance was given in the removal of wounded soldiers and officers from the Hospital Ships, when required.

During the critical period of Rebellion our three ambulances were worked continuously in removing the wounded under great difficulty and constant peril from stray bullets, on many occasions being under actual fire ; one of the horses was shot through the foreleg. In addition, many other humanitarian services were rendered, such as bringing food and doctors to an hospital otherwise inaccessible, and removing sick persons from danger zones to places of greater safety, etc.

Since its establishment the following number of calls were received for the ambulance :—

1899	–	537 calls	13	private cases.
1900	–	660 ,,	21	,,
1901	–	808 ,,	43	,,
1902	–	1,090 ,,	39	,,
1903	–	1,295 ,,	53	,,
1904	–	1,266 ,,	50	,,
1905	–	1,605 ,,	91	,,
1906	–	1,738 ,,	102	,,
1907	–	1,780 ,,	84	,,
1908	–	1,718 ,,	108	,,
1909	–	1,518 ,,	106	,,
1910	–	1,691 ,,	120	,,
1911	–	1,902 ,,	126	,,

21

1912	–	1,823 calls	93	private cases
1913	–	2,206 ,,	87	,,
1914	–	2,530 ,,	102	,,
1915	–	2,126 ,,	90	,,
1916	–	2,331 ,,	68	,,

The annexed Table C, page 25, gives the cases tabulated by days, months, and causes.

PLANT (in Service).

1 Steam Fire Engine, capacity 800 gallons per min.

1 do. do. 300 do.

2 Petrol Motor Pumps. 350 to 800 do.

3 Aerial Extension Ladders, 66 feet elevation, with water tower apparatus.

2 Hose Tenders, with accessories, including folding Pompier Ladders.

1 Hose Wagon.

1 Motor Ambulance.

2 Ambulance Wagons.

1 Trap for Chief Officer.

8 Horses.

3 Telescopic Ladders, 28 feet extension.

7 Jumping Sheets and Life Lines.

12 Hand Pumps.

18 Stand Pipes.

25 Branch Pipes.

2 Cellar Pipes.

11,600 Feet $2\frac{3}{4}$-inch Canvas Hose.

80 do. Leather do.

100 Feet $3\frac{1}{2}$-inch Canvas Hose.

1 Smoke Helmet, " Bader Patent."

1 Oxygen Rescue Apparatus.

22

(In Reserve).

1 " Clayton " Fire Escape, with fore-carriage and shafts, 72 feet elevation.

1 Hose Tender.

2 Hand Hose Carts.

1 General Purpose Wagonette.

10 Stand Pipes.

2 Branch Pipes.

Total value of Plant and Furniture, £8,873.

No additions have been made to the plant, which was kept carefully examined and all necessary repairs executed.

FACTORY AND WORKSHOPS ACT.

All matters relating to exits as provided by this Act received attention.

Tabulated returns are submitted showing :—

A.—Means by which alarms were received, their classification and distribution, property at risk, and losses for each month during the year.

B.—The number of fires. Risk and losses for each of the past twenty years.

C.—Ambulance cases classified.

THOMAS P. PURCELL,
Chief Superintendent.

Chief Fire Station,
Dublin, *February 26th*, 1917.

23

TABLE A.

1916.	FIRES IN CITY — Serious damage	FIRES IN CITY — Medium damage	FIRES IN CITY — Slight damage	FIRES IN CITY — Chimney fires	Calls outside City	To Fallen Houses etc.	False alarms	BRIGADE TURNED OUT — Day	BRIGADE TURNED OUT — Night	HOW CALLS WERE RECEIVED — Verbally	HOW CALLS WERE RECEIVED — By Telephone	HOW CALLS WERE RECEIVED — May Oatway Automatic	HOW CALLS WERE RECEIVED — Telegram	HOW CALLS WERE RECEIVED — Street Fire Alarms	Total number of Fires and Alarms	TOTAL AMOUNT AT RISK. £	TOTAL LOSS IN CITY. £	LOSS not insured (included in Total). £
TOTALS	4	13	83	23	7	3	12	42	51	32	81			31	145	465,733	41,209	50
January	1		14	5			5	2	14	3	14			8	25	24,883	7,954	2
February	1	2	11	3				5	5	2	11			4	17	115,703	2,805	5
March	1		5	4			1	2	4	4	8				12	52,287	806	
April *		1	6	3	ship	1	1	3	1	3	6			1	9	4,100	34	21
May		1	11	1			3	2	4	3	6			5	10	5,850	431	
June	1		6			1		6	4	2	9			2	17	125,100	27,722	2
July			5					3	3	3	2			1	7	8,260	57	15
August		1	4	2	1			1	2	4	1			1	6	54,010	17	
September		1	5	1	1	1		1	3	2	5			1	8	14,510	63	1
October		3	5	1	2			5	4	2	6			1	9	44,200	224	
November		3	5	1	1	1		5	4	4	9			2	11	11,430	938	
December		2	6	3	1		2	7	4	4	4			6	14	5,400	158	4

* In addition the conflagrations due to Rebellion not included.

135

24

TABLE B.

Amount of property at risk and damaged by fires in the Borough of Dublin, which were attended by the Brigade during the previous twenty years :—

Year.	No. of Fires in City each year.	Estimated Amount of Property at Risk in each Year.	Estimated Total Amount Destroyed in each Year.	Destroyed and not Insured (Estimated) included in Total.
		£	£	£
1896	132	404,483	25,816	1,358
1897	120	201,900	9,920	487
1898	142	1,000,615	37,676	370
1899	159	458,051	20,821	550
1900	121	402,120	9,343	452
1901	127	910,323	27,770	423
1902	149	639,384	*129,551	1,304
1903	133	1,351,572	11,131	1,166
1904	154	530,999	14,351	437
1905	162	770,733	29,779	234
1906	131	679,198	10,508	783
1907	162	971,092	57,607	1,970
1908	148	631,861	92,066	215
1909	131	373,051	30,987	870
1910	133	474,390	27,695	523
1911	164	345,742	8,487	447
1912	147	771,757	26,483	466
1913	146	388,268	20,070	174
1914	164	921,306	15,650	373
1915	161	635,584	41,981	253
Total	2,886	12,862,429	637,702	12,854
Average Previous 20 Years.	144·3	643,121	31,385	642
1916	†100	465,733	41,209	50

* Todds.   † Fires due to Rebellion not included

TABLE C.

AMBULANCE.

1916.

Category	Total
Wounds.	301
Weakness.	197
Unconscious.	63
Throats Cut.	8
Sprains.	23
Spinal Injuries.	17
Shock.	19
Scalp Wounds.	137
Recovered on arrival.	108
Patient sick in bed, not removed.	112
Private Cases	89
Poisoning.	8
Otherwise removed.	159
Other Injuries.	345
Not available.	7
Internal Injuries.	23
Hemorrhage.	27
Gas Poisoning.	2
Fractures (Lr. limbs).	69
Fractures (Upr. limbs).	20
Fits—Fainting.	140
Fits—Epileptic.	273
Drowning.	25
Dislocations.	10
Dead on arrival.	23
Cramps.	24
Confinement in street.	35
Concussions.	4
Burns.	13
Bruises.	21

Days.	Dec.	Nov.	Oct.	Sept.	August	July	June	May	April	Mar.	Feb.	Jan.	Total
	189	161	195	214	171	232	203	217	314	135	140	160	2,331
Sunday	31	12	20	29	13	23	15	13	20	6	7	16	205
Monday	22	21	33	32	33	41	30	45	57	22	34	32	402
Tuesday	28	25	21	30	25	23	34	50	57	13	26	20	352
Wednesday	22	24	29	30	23	27	16	36	49	14	18	21	309
Thursday	16	27	32	26	23	27	32	23	51	32	16	13	318
Friday	28	20	21	20	23	28	29	19	47	25	12	19	291
Saturday	42	32	39	47	31	63	47	31	33	23	27	39	454
Total,	...	...	...	...	...	...	...	...	...	...	...	...	

26

APPENDIX.

———

PARTICULARS OF ALL FIRES WITHIN THE CITY WHERE THE LOSS EXCEEDED £50.

———

1. *January* 10*th*.—8 Ormond Quay, at 2.23 a.m., by 'phone. Owners, John McDonnel and Co., Ltd., Paper manufacturers. Cause unknown. Originated on ground floor about centre of premises, 25 feet frontage, depth 140 feet, four and five floors over basement, and had extended through whole of ground floor and all the upper floors of storage portion at rear before being discovered; four families occupying two upper floors in front over warehouse made their escape by the stairs. Extinguished at 5.46 a.m. by four jets from hydrant. Contents of warehouse and office badly damaged, stores destroyed. Insurance, £8,500. Loss, £7,880.

2. *February* 8*th*.—South Brown Street, at 1.54 p.m., by 'phone. Owners, Irish Curled Hair Co., Bedding Factory. Cause unknown. Originated in a store 40 by 18 at N.W. corner of factory. Removed portion of contents, and extinguished by one jet from hydrant augmented by motor. Insurance, £7,800. Loss, £250.

3. *February* 9*th*.—Rogerson's Quay, at 4.06 a.m., by 'phone. Owners, Paul and Vincent, Fertiliser Manufacturers. Cause, spontaneous ignition of rags. Originated on upper floor of a two-storied building used for storage. Extinguished at 5.59 a.m. by four jets from motors, taking suction from river. The roof and contents of portion, 60 x 25, with L extension of 40 feet, destroyed. Insurance, £65,800. Loss, £2,460.

4. *February* 18*th*.—24 St. Andrew Street, at 11.17 a.m., by 'phone. In the offices on top floor, occupied by Little and Cullen, Solicitors. Originated within a press. Extinguished at 12.21 p.m. by one jet from hydrant and hand pump. Insurance, £1,200. Loss, £55.

5. *March* 1*st*.—Rear 32-34 Abbey Street, Upper, at 5.12 a.m., by 'phone. In a Cabinet Factory. Owners, T. R. Scott and Co. Originated in the Diesel Engine room, containing 20 barrels crude oil. Forced entrance and extinguished by one jet from

27

hydrant at 6.47 a.m.; glazed enclosure and portion of roof destroyed; works saved. Insurance, £13,200. Loss, £206.

6. *March 13th.*—At Island Bridge, at 1.20 p.m., by 'phone. Owners, Plunkett Bros., Maltsters. Cause, ignition of combings. Originated in a drying kiln. Extinguished by one jet from motor. Roof ventilator destroyed. Insurance, £26,000. Loss, £67.

7. *March 23rd.*—16 Crow Street, at 8.06 p.m., by 'phone. Occupier, Arthur Shifts, Tailor. Cause unknown. Originated beneath counter in shop; forced entrance. Extinguished by jet from hydrant at 8.46 p.m. Insurance, £1,200. Loss, £500.

8. *May 11th.*—1 Wentworth Place, at 10.34 p.m., by 'phone. Owner, H. V. Parkinson, Chandler and Oil Shop. Originated from an unknown cause in shop beneath a four-storied building. Extinguished at 11.11 p.m. by two jets from hydrants. Insurance, £950. Loss, £420.

9. *June 10th.*—At 114 Stephen's Green, at 5 p.m., by Box 71. Owners, Jones and Sons, Decorators and Contractors. Cause unknown. The fire originated in a building, 90 x 25, at rear of main building, used as offices, show-room, and stores, which was fully alight, and had extended to Kapp and Peterson's pipe factory adjoining. The stores, with stocks of turpentine, oils, varnish, etc., were destroyed, but workshop and front portion of premises saved.

Kapp and Peterson's large stock of materials and finished goods were destroyed, but factory and plant saved. Both establishments had been closed from 1 p.m. Roof of Unitarian Church adjoining on South side damaged; stained glass window destroyed, organ and church furniture damaged by smoke and water.

Extinguished by six jets from hydrants, pressure augmented by motor. Jones and Sons' Insurance, £8,600. Loss, £5,100. Kapp and Peterson's Insurance, £20,500. Loss, £18,500. Church, £7,600. Loss, £3,900.

10. *June 29th.*—Newmarket, at 4.30 a.m., by 'phone. Owners, P. R. Norton and Co., Maltsters. Originated in a malt-bin, 12 x 12, on top floor. Extinguished at 5.53 a.m. by one jet from hydrant. Portion of bin and roof damaged. Insurance, £3,000. Loss, about £200.

11. *September 16th.*—Stephen's Green, 134 and 135. Alexandra Club, at 11.19 p.m., by Box 71. Originated within a wardrobe

28

in a top back bedroom. Extinguished by hand pump. Insurance, £1,600. Loss, £60.

12. *October 15th.*—Wellington Quay, at 4.07 p.m., by 'phone. Owners, Clarence Hotel Co. Originated in a timber and vulcanite roof over kitchen. Cause, timber built into flue. Extinguished at 5.03 p.m. by one jet from hydrant. Insurance, £5,000. Loss, £110.

13. *November 9th.*—46 Harrington Street, at 1.24 a.m., by Box 66. Occupier, Max Cowan. Trading as Franco-British Art Co. Cause unascertained. Forced entrance and extinguished four square yards of first and second floors, used as work-rooms and stores, at 2.45 a.m., by one jet from hydrant. Insurance, £1,200. Loss, £620. Two firemen, shocked by a live electric wire, fell from first floor window to street; one of them was injured about face.

14. *November 16th.*—14 Suffolk Street, at 2.17 a.m., by 'phone. Occupier, J. L. Dixon, Cycle Agent. Cause unknown. Forced entrance and found shop and room above on fire. Extinguished at 3.30 a.m. by one jet from hydrant. Insurance, £150. Loss, £190.

15. *November 16th.*—36 Usher's Quay, at 9.30 p.m., by Box 96. Owners, Petrie Bros., Sack Manufacturers. Roof and floor of store, with quantity of sacks, damaged and destroyed. Insurance, £1,800. Loss, £112.

16. *December 7th.*—16 Wicklow Street, at 3.53 a.m., by 'phone. Occupier, Charles Milne. Originated from unknown cause in a tailor's workroom on first floor. Forced entrance and extinguished by jet from hydrant at 4.42 a.m. Portion of floor, 8 x 4, and some stationery on ground floor, destroyed. Insurance, £800. Loss, £100.

17. *December 17th.*—163 Great Brunswick Street, at 10.43 p.m. Owner, Mrs. Preston. Cause, defective construction. Forced entrance, removed hearth, and extinguished joists, etc., in back drawingroom. Insurance, £1,500. Loss, £50.

THOMAS P. PURCELL,

CENTRAL FIRE STATION,   *Chief Officer.*
  DUBLIN, *January,* 1917.

Dollard—K—3972 3. 1917.—   Irish Paper,

APPENDIX E

STATISTICS

OF THE

DUBLIN CORPORATION

FIRE BRIGADE DEPARTMENT

FOR

THIRTY-FOUR YEARS,

FROM ITS FORMATION SEPTEMBER, 1862, TO
31ST DECEMBER, 1895,

WITH

*Statement of Work done, Income, Expenditure, Averages, and other
Information pertinent to the extension of the Brigade, for which
powers are sought by Improvement Bill 59 and 60 Victoria,
Session, 1896.*

COMPILED 1ST APRIL, 1896.

THOMAS P. PURCELL,
Chief Superintendent.

DOLLARD, PRINTINGHOUSE, DUBLIN.
1896.

3

DUBLIN CORPORATION FIRE BRIGADE.

The City of Dublin comprise an area of 3,808 acres, or about 6 square miles, and about 133 miles of streets within the municipal boundary; the number of houses which, in 1881 was 27,557, had increased to 29,524 in 1891, and is still increasing each year; the valuation for Public Water Rate, in 1861, was £529,543 15s.; in 1881, £651,064; and in 1895 it had increased to £692,439 10s., or an increase of 30·76 per cent. The population which, in 1861, was 254,808, and in 1881, 249,602, was reduced in 1891 to 245,001.

EARLY HISTORY OF BRIGADE.

For some years prior to 1862, in consequence of the frequency with which lives were lost at fires, a local society, supported by voluntary contributions acting in connection with " The Royal Society for Protection of Life from Fire," maintained 7 Life Escapes in the vicinity of churches, and provided men in charge of them. But the responsibilities of extinguishing fires or saving property did not properly rest with any particular organization. The Corporation possessed a Manual Engine, and the men who worked it being employed at their respective trades during the day, and residing in different parts of the city, were not very effective. An engine was also placed in charge of the police. Several Fire Insurance Companies and parishes had small engines which were not of much practical use; the divided efforts of these bodies were not satisfactory, and the loss, by fire, was very considerable.

4

Brigade Established.

Such were the conditions prevailing when, in 1862, the Corporation, under the guidance of the late lamented Sir John Gray, promoted their Fire Brigade Act, and, under the powers thus obtained, establised a permanent Fire Department, with paid men, and improved appliances, in charge of a Superintendent. The Life Escapes were also purchased and taken over from the Society, and the Brigade devoted its whole time to the saving of life and property within the city.

Results of Working.

As a result of organization, better appliances, increased watchfulness and strength, the average loss which, at first, was over 50 per cent. of the property exposed to fire, was steadily reduced until it stands at 13·8 for the past five years, and 20·1 per cent. for the whole period of 34 years covered by the work of Department. The Brigade attended 9,612 fires. The total amount of property exposed to risk was estimated to be value for £4,818,098, and the total loss ascertained to be £968,700 (see tables herewith). During the same period the number of Escapes was gradually increased from 7 to 12, and in 1882 the Conductors were put in direct telephonic communication with the Fire Stations. The number of lives actually rescued by the Brigade without having suffered permanent injury are 100, and the lives lost at fires number 33, many of them were rescued but died in hospital afterwards. Three members of the Brigade were killed while engaged at fires.

In addition to fires in the city each year, assistance was sought by owners of property in the surrounding Townships and County of Dublin. Under the 9th

5

Clause of Fire Brigade Act a portion of the Brigade, with engines and appliances, was permitted to attend 129 fires outside the city, and in many cases succeeded in saving much valuable property. Notably, in 1878, £60,000 at Maynooth College, 15 miles distant; in 1894, £33,000 at Artane Industrial School, 3½ miles; and in 1895, at Oil Refinery, Dunsinea, 5 miles distant, £16,000 was saved from destruction.—See Reports, published annually, for details of work performed.

NECESSITY FOR ENLARGEMENT AND BETTER DISTRIBUTION OF THE FORCE.

Up to 1890 the Brigade numbered less than 40 men and officers. In that year, owing to the construction of lope-line bridges, a considerable portion of the city was cut off from the ordinary service of Life Escapes, two new Stations had to be established North and South of the river entailing an increase of eight men to the Department.

Since the Brigade was established the city has been opened up and expanded towards the boundary, and many new streets added. Besides the enlargement and increased value of property in the city, the character of buildings and nature of contents has considerably altered; the tendency to remove walls, open up and enlarge shops, warehouses, &c., increase stocks, including those of light materials and volatile substances, and a more general application of artificial means of heating and lighting, together with, perhaps, greater carelessness in their use, has undoubtedly enlarged the risks from fire and increased their number. The principals and responsible managers of business and trade, who formerly resided either in a part of the same building or in the immediate vicinity of their offices or warehouses, now live away in the townships

6

at a distance, and the premises being locked up at night accidental smouldering fires often go on unnoticed and unchecked until they have gained a considerable hold on the building, and then require a strong force of Firemen to cope with or prevent their spread to surrounding property.

There are 15 men engaged every night on escape duty and in charge of public buildings, so that without making allowance for illness, accident, or men on leave, but 28, including officers, are available for fires at night when most needed ; this number, while inadequate to deal with a large fire, leave no reserve to attend to a second outbreak which has not infrequently occurred, in another portion of the City at same time.

At present the whole force is located at Chatham-row and Winetavern-street, both stations near centre of city, but most of the North side and portions of the South are very far removed from protection, several sections being nearly two miles from the nearest station. The Brigade has no proper enclosed yard for drilling or training purposes. The space previously available at Winetavern-street is now crowded out by the working of other Corporation Departments ; the premises are altogether unsuitable either for a quick " turn out " or keeping the apparatus in proper condition, and the men living away in tenement rooms, a distance from the station, cannot be under proper control. The station at Chatham-row requires a better outlet, by having a block of unsanitary tenement houses in front removed, and the building otherwise enlarged and remodelled. In order that more immediate relief and prompter attendance to calls be given in every part of the city the Force requires to be better distributed in compact stations on suitable thoroughfares, as set forth in Report No. 107—1895, which received the assent of the Council.

A proper system of public electrical fire alarms are required for use at night when telephones are not generally available.

NECESSITY FOR INCREASED FUNDS.

At first, for want of funds, the Brigade was established in two temporary stations at William-street and White-horse-yard in a portion of premises which were the property of the Corporation and used for other purposes. It was always the intention of the promoters—(see Water-works Report, No.   )—that when funds permitted, the complete organization should be located in and directed from a proper Central Station, with four branch stations in the different divisions of the city. But it was found the sum allocated from Public Water Rate of 1½d. in the £, which fell to 1d. in 1873, was only sufficient to meet current expenses of maintenance, renewal of plant, &c., and no surplus remained with which to build stations until after 1874, when power was given by Provisional Order Act to allocate one-half the Public Water Rate for Brigade purposes – the sum not to exceed 1½d. in the £.

In 1885 the new station at Chatham-row was built and equipped, at a cost of £5,564 4s. 6d., out of Brigade funds, and the premises at William-street given up. The Domestic Water Rate having been reduced from 1s. to 6d., and Public Water Rate to 1½d., the income therefrom being insufficient to maintain the Brigade it became necessary to amend the provisions existing, and by the Dublin Corporation Act of 1890 the Public Water Rate was again fixed at 3d., the Brigade getting one-half the assessment.

Annexed tables gives the total amounts received from the several sources and expended on the Brigade for the

8

whole period since its formation, in 1862, to 31st December, 1895, including £1,400 17s. 4d., the cost of obtaining the Act, and £795 12s. compensation to the families of three Firemen who were killed, the total amount paid was £131,177 7s. 11d. The value of buildings owned by Department is £6,500, and plant £6,394, with a balance to credit of £3,089 3s. 4d.

No contribution, donation, or annual subscription has been received from Insurance or other Companies, or individuals, as contemplated by the 11th Clause of Fire Brigade Act. The income for whole period was £134,266 11s. 3d., the average being £3,949 0s. 4d. per year, while the expenditure was £3,858 3s. 2d.

Since the Brigade was increased to its present strength, and wages of men raised, the average income was £4,925 2s. 6d., and the yearly expenditure, £5,734 16s. 6d., being an excess over income of £809 14s. per annum, for past five years. While the average excess expenditure over proportion of income received from Public Water Rate has been £1,236 2s. yearly.

AVERAGES FOR WHOLE PERIOD, FIRST AND LAST FIVE YEARS.

Average	Strength of Brigade	No. of Fires	Property at Risk			Property Lost			Income			Expenditure		
			£	s.	d.	£	s.	d.	£	s.	d.	£	s.	d.
For First 5 Years ..	29	174	46,675	12	0	23,508	18	8	3 070	13	9	3,503	19	9
For Whole Period ...	30·6	282·7	141,708	15	6	28,491	3	8	3,949	0	4	3,858	3	2
For Last 5 Years ...	47	336	412,579	8	0	57,086	14	1	4,925	2	6	5,734	16	6

9

Names of Men and Officers who Died in the Fire Brigade Service since its Formation in September, 1862, to 31st December, 1895.

No.	Name and Rank	Dates of Joining	Dates of Death	Length of Service, Years	Remarks
1	Fireman Michael Murphy ...	Oct. 11, 1862	March 16, 1864	1½	Consumption
2	,, John Graydon ..	,, ,,	May 22, 1865	2½	Typhus Fever
3	,, William Madden ...	Dec. 8, 1862	May 28, 1868	5½	Consumption
4	,, Richard Byrne ...	June 6, 1865	March 2, 1867	2	,,
5	,, Joseph Hayes ...	April 25, 1868	June 4, 1869	1	,,
6	Inspector Andrew Cowan ...	Aug. 30, 1868	Aug. 26, 1873	5	,,
7	Captain T. R. Ingram ...	Sept. 1862	May 15, 1882	19⅔	,,
8	Fireman Patrick Lee ...	Oct. 17, 1862	Aug. 25, 1882	20	Old Age and Debility
9	,, John Purcell ...	May 4, 1870	April 1, 1883	13	Consumption
10	,, Thomas Whelan ...	Sept. 26, 1873	Sept. 11, 1887	14	,,
11	Inspector John Hines ...	Sept. 14, 1869	April 15, 1888	18¼	General Debility
12	Engineer Mathew Waddell ...	Dec. 10, 1864	June 16, 1892	27½	,, ,,
13	Fireman Robert Haddeway	Feb. 1, 1876	March 30, 1894	18	,, ,,

Names of Men who have been Killed while Working at Fires or Died of their Injuries, since Formation, September, 1862.
Families Compensated.

No.	Names	Date of Joining	Date of Death	Years Service	Remarks
1	John Kite	Jan. 3, 1877 ...	March 20, 1884	6¾	Killed at fire, 10 Trinity-st. (Collapsing of building).
2	Peter Burke	March 23, 1891	May 20, 1891	¼	Killed at fire, 30 Westmore-land-street
3	Inspector Christopher Doherty	Sept. 3, 1868 ...	May 20, 1891		Killed at fire, 30 Westmore-land-street (Collapse No. 4 Life Escape).

10

NAMES OF MEN WHO HAVE BEEN FOUND MEDICALLY UNFIT FOR SERVICE AND WERE DISCHARGED.

No.	Names	Dates of Joining	Dates of Discharge	Years Service	Remarks
1	Henry Goodfellow ...	... Jan. 5, 1871 ...	Feb. 25, 1871	...	Defective Sight
2	James Moylan ...	... April 3, 1871	Sept. 23, 1877	6½	Consumption
3	Thomas Dunne, 1st ...	... Feb. 28, 1877	Feb. 5, 1881...	4	Committed to Lunatic Asylum
4	Thomas Dunne, 2nd...	... May 30, 1881	Aug. 12, 1882	1¼	Consumption
5	Patrick Hammond ...	... Aug. 27, 1889	Dec. 11, 1891	2¼	do.
6	Sylvester M'Sweeny	... July 20, 1890...	July 22, 1893...	3	do.

NAMES OF MEN IN THE SERVICE WHO WOULD NOW BE ENTITLED TO SUPERANNUATION, IF THE PROVISIONS OF LOCAL OFFICERS' SUPERANNUATION ACT WERE EXTENDED TO INCLUDE WORKMEN.

No.	Names	Date of Joining	Rank	Years Service	Cause	
1	Henry Blake ...	... July 6, 1866 ...	Fireman	...29¾	Old Age and Infirmity	
2	Michael Gaines ...	... April 16, 1867	Do.	... 29	do.	do.
3	William Myers ...	... April 24, 1871	Inspector	... 25	do.	do.
4	Richard Cullen ...	... Oct. 17, 1871	Fireman	...24½	do.	do.

11

Extracts from Acts.

"For the purpose of providing a supply of water for better security against fire, for flushing sewers, for public baths and wash-houses, for drinking fountains, and for sanitary uses," the Corporation is empowered by the Dublin Corporation Waterworks Act, 1861 (24 and 25 Vic., cap. 172, Local Sec. 56), to levy from the owners of rateable property, a Public Water Rate of one-fourth part of the amount in the £ of the Domestic Water Rate, which rate is not to exceed one shilling.

By the Dublin Corporation Act of 1890, the restriction as to the Public Water Rate not exceeding one-fourth of the Domestic Water Rate, has been removed, and the Corporation can now levy the full amount of 3d., irrespective of what the Domestic Rate may be.

The Dublin Corporation Fire Brigade Act of 1862, as amended by the Local Government Board (Ireland) Provisional Order Act of 1874 prescribes, that the amount of the Public Water Rate to be appropriated for the purposes of that Act—"the extinguishing of fires, and protection of life and property against fire is not to exceed 1½d. in the £."

The adoption of Report No. 107, 1895, and the carrying out of the improvements mentioned therein, will entail a capital expenditure of say, £12,500, and an increased charge for maintenance of about £600.

One 1d. in the £ on the valuation of £692,439, on which the Public Water Rate has been assessed, would produce:—

	£2,885
2d. in the £	£5,770
3d. in the £	£8,655
½d. in the £	£1,442

12

The quantity of water used for the purpose of extinguishing fires, flushing sewers, public baths and wash-houses, for drinking fountains and sanitary purposes, that is to say, the other purposes to which the Public Water Rate is applicable has been estimated at 204,000,000 gallons for the current year, which, at $2\frac{1}{2}$d. per 1,000 gallons, amounts to £2,125,

A reference to the Estimate for the Public Water Rate for the year 1895, will show how this amount, £2,125, which is transferred from the Domestic Water Rate Estimate to the Public Water Rate Estimate, is dealt with in calculating the amount required to be assessed for levying Public Water Rate.

APPENDIX F

7. Melrose av. Fairview
16th Feby. 06.

Dear O'Hara,

I have your letter of the 16th inst. informing me of the apology tendered by the Captain to Giffney and the men, and the consequent ending of the case. I send you herewith copy of the letter I had prepared to send in to the committee on the day fixed; and I may here say that the Captain by your acceptance of his apology, has barely escaped public censure, if not dismissal from his post. As is usual with such matters, the Captain came to hear that the men were making a stand, that I had the matter in hands, and that I had documents and witnesses

ready for proof. He also heard that
I was about the City Hall on Tuesday
relating the facts and showing
the documents to members of the
Council. This apparently brought
him to his knees, for on the
evening of that day, a gentleman
whom I know to be fairly intimate
with the Captain called in to me
at the College with the object of
endeavouring to settle matters, both
for Siffney's sake as well as for the
Captain's. I related to this gentleman the whole history of the matter
as well as former cases, and read to
him the copy of enclosed letter.
I stated that unless some reparation
were made, the men were determined
to proceed; and advised him to
see the Captain, tell him all that I knew
and inform him of the documents
and proofs I purposed using in

the case. The gentleman I refer to evidently did as I suggested, hence the apology. It is perhaps as well the matter ended in this way — especially for the Captain. And I am glad to know he is aware that I have a rod in pickle for him should he be again guilty of tyranny or brutality towards any member of the Brigade.

I hope the matter will prove to the men the value of a little pluck, back-bone, and united action when dealing with any man — no matter how high-placed — who tries to act the tyrant and the bully over his fellows.

I presume you will inform all the men of the results of this case, and how they were brought about.

Yrs truly Th. Richardson